SUCCESSFUL
DELEGATION

SUCCESSFUL
DELEGATION

THE HASSLE-FREE WAY TO GET
OTHER PEOPLE TO WORK
FOR EVERYONE'S BENEFIT

BY

BILL TRUBY
JOANN TRUBY

EDITED BY W. A. NEWMAN

TRUBY ACHIEVEMENT CENTER
MOUNT SHASTA, CALIFORNIA

SUCCESSFUL DELEGATION
Bill & Joann Truby

Published by Angel's Dream Publishing Company
P.O. Box 1440
Mt. Shasta, California 96067
Tel; Fax; Pager: 877-377-3279

Find us on the World Wide Web at: www.trubyachievementcenter.com

Cover design:
Interior design and illustrations: William A. Newman and
    Wordsmiths Marketing

Colophon
This book was created with Adobe InDesign 2.0 on a Macintosh G3.
The body text is set in Adobe Garamond; illustration captions are set in
Arial, and title pages are set in Copperplate Gothic.

ISBN 0-9725897-0-8
Printed and bound in the United States of America by LSI

DEDICATION

To our sons …
where we learned to let go
so they could become men.

Bill and Joann

vi

TABLE OF CONTENTS

PREFACE

"Forget it! I'm not about to pass responsibility for this project to someone else when I *know* it will not be done right."

Have you ever said or thought this? Of course you have. We all have at one time in our life or another. The simple fact is most busy, accomplished people have given up on delegating for that very reason. Yet, there are heavy costs to you when you try to do it all yourself: costs to your effectiveness in your job, costs to your relationships in your family, and costs to your health and psychological well-being.

But there is an answer. Delegation does not have to be the trap most people think it is. The Successful Delegation System, a simple process we've been teaching and using at the Truby Achievement Center for many years, can free you to use your time more effectively, be more productive, and enjoy your life more.

Later in this book, you'll learn how successful delegation can ...

- leverage your time and effort as much as 6,000% (we'll show you in a later chapter how this phenomenal leverage is possible);
- increase trust among your coworkers;
- improve you bottom line;
- build team dynamics, and
- create improvement.

The first step is to read this short book. And when you learn the five simple steps to successful delegation, you'll be able to bring this sort of leverage into your life almost effortlessly ... because you will be able to get other people to work effectively for everyone's benefit.

CHAPTER 1

"ASK A BUSY PERSON"

If you picked up this book to read, you are undoubtedly the "Go To" person in your organization. You know what we mean. You are the person who people trust to get things done thoroughly, competently, and on time.

Or perhaps, you are on your way to becoming that person. Maybe you have recently been promoted or moved into a position in your organization where now you will be managing projects and the activities of other people because a supervisor or manager recognizes previously untapped people-management skills and abilities in you that you are now going to have to use.

Regardless of why or how you have reached this position of responsibility for the actions of other people and the outcomes you hope to get from them, two things are certain:

YOUR LIFE IS FULL, PROFESSIONALLY AND PERSONALLY ... AND YOU REALLY LIKE IT THAT WAY.

But you are beginning to realize your life is getting a bit too full. It is time to pull back, slow down, not take on so much responsibility in your life.

So just about the time you are saying to yourself, "I'm not able to take on anymore in my life," it invariably happens. Your boss, your Rotary Club President, the City Manager, your pastor, or some other person comes to you and says, "I've got this project that's right up your alley. You'll be perfect for it."

And you know what? They are right. The project is one you are perfect for, one that you would love to "put your stamp on," so you readjust your schedule and take it on.

Sound familiar? If you feel beset and besieged by demands on you … if you wish there were 36 hours in a day and 9 days in a week … if you are torn between family, work, and social obligations … this book was written so that you can put your stamp on projects important to you while maintaining balance among the important aspects of your life.

12

"IF YOU WANT TO GET SOMETHING DONE WELL … ASK A BUSY PERSON."

How many times have you heard this cliché applied directly to you? When your boss brings you a new assignment and you try to beg off, you know this is exactly what she will say. And it is true. Busy people such as you are the ones who get things done correctly and on time.

However, there is often a cost extracted from your life because of it. You have been there, I am sure, when you feel you cannot add one more item to your plate without seriously impacting the quality of work in all of your projects or, worse, the quality of your life.

How do you handle those times? How do *most* people in your position handle those times? You do not say, "No." That is simply not your way of doing things. And sometimes it's even impossible to say "no" … and still keep your job.

So you do the same thing most busy, committed people do in this situation. You take on the additional commitment and shuffle your other responsibilities around.

What is the cost to you when you do more than you ought to be doing?

- Your stress level increases dramatically;
- Your productivity drops significantly;
- Your family life suffers;
- Your personal relationships deteriorate;
- And the joy you should be feeling in your accomplishments—the joy you felt in the past that was a prime motivator for you—simply is no longer there.

What replaces that joy? A feeling of being used by those around you. A feeling of inadequacy in your life. A feeling of chasing yourself and not getting anything of importance accomplished. A feeling of depression and anger.

Just like Alice in Wonderland during the caucus race, you end up feeling like you are running in circles without getting anywhere.

13

Figure 1 – The Caucus Race Syndrome
Run. Run. Run.
The faster we run, the farther behind we get

ESCAPE THE CAUCUS RACE ...
AND SAVE THE QUALITY OF YOUR LIFE

There is a way out of this predicament. And as you know, it is not by saying, "no." The solution is one that is far harder for most goal-oriented people such as you to do than saying "no." That solution is:

> Delegating responsibility ... so that *you* can work more efficiently, more effectively, with less stress and strain on your relationships

14

We know full well what you are thinking right now. "Whenever I try to delegate authority, nothing gets done right. I end up having to do it all myself anyway, so why delegate in the first place?"

There are some very good reasons why things do not get done properly when people delegate. Fortunately for you and other over-extended people, the problems that prevent efficient delegation are easy to understand ... and easy to fix.

Our work over the past twenty-years with people has been based on an over-riding principle: human and organizational behavior can be broken down into basic principles that define and determine that behavior. This is true whether you examine the functioning of a large multinational corporation or the interactions that occur when you delegate a simple task to someone in your local service or social club.

In this book there is a system of principles and methodologies that, if adopted and followed completely, is destined to give you success in delegation—success you can see and measure. This process works!

Typical success results include higher morale—both yours and the person or people to whom you delegated, better attitudes, greater productivity and —if you are in business—increased profits. The process gives you these results because we have, over many years, built on what works and eliminated what does not work. This has resulted in a proven series of steps that brings measurable success.

This short book will show you exactly how to apply these basic principles of human and organizational interaction so that you can delegate effectively and successfully. Here is what you will learn as you go through this book:

- Chapter 2 will go over the reasons why it is so important for you to be able to delegate effectively.
- Chapters 3 through 6 get down to the "nitty gritty" of how to delegate effectively. In these chapters, you will learn those basic principles of human interaction that can prevent effective delegation if they are not fully understood. You will also learn how to apply these principles so that you and your teammates will benefit.
- Chapter 7 is a brief discussion on ways to delegate: delegating down (the most common), delegating sideways, and delegating up.
- Chapter 8 examines threats to successful delegation, both those that come from outside and those that come from within you. By knowing where the pitfalls and barriers to effective delegation lie, you will be able to avoid them before they stop you.
- Chapter 9 presents a brief summary of what you have learned.
- Lastly, Chapter 10 is a glossary of terms.

15

At the beginning of every chapter, you will find a brief outline of what you should expect to learn in the chapter. At the end of each chapter, I will give you a *brief* summary of what was presented. Words that are listed in the Glossary are underlined.

None of what is presented in these pages is difficult. The power comes when you delegate cleanly and clearly. The magic comes when you put this system into practice in the sequence we suggest. People you delegate to are magically transformed into "owners" of their tasks or projects *wanting* to perform successfully for their own satisfaction and the good of the whole. And, yes, this *can* be done!

There is no reason why you should continue in your solo quest to hold the earth on your shoulders like a latter day Atlas. This book will show you how to get the load off of your shoulders so that you can be more successful in every aspect of your life ... and get pleasure from more joy in your life.

It is certainly worth a try. If you learn how to delegate effectively, you might just live longer since you will have reduced the stress in your life considerably. But we can guarantee, you will live happier.

16

Figure 2 – You don't have to carry the world on your shoulders. Learn how to delegate effectively, and others will share a much more manageable load.

CHAPTER 2
DELEGATION: HIGH IMPACT LEVERAGE

In this chapter you will learn:

- Why it is important to delegate responsibility
- The personal cost of not delegating
- How delegating helps improve business and social relationships
- How delegation provides leverage for your time and improves your effectiveness
- How lack of delegation will produce "inverse leverage" to your detriment

17

Why should you delegate when the results usually are so dismal and the process seems so ineffective? We have already touched on a few reasons why it is important for busy people to learn to delegate in Chapter 1. These are personal and business reasons, reasons that have to do with productivity, effectiveness ... and reasons having to do with your personal life. To expand on those reasons, let us look at a real story about a real person who had difficulty with delegation and so decided to "do it all himself."

HOW MUCH OF YOUR LIFE CAN YOU AFFORD TO GIVE AWAY?

We will call my friend George. He lives in a community in the mountains of far northern California. George is one of those people like you, a "go-to person." When things need to be done, people go to him to get them done. Several years ago, George was president of a local service club. The job contained a great many responsibilities, some of which George had undertaken prior to becoming president and some of which were new for the year.

One of the new responsibilities was organizing an annual triathlon that was a long-time fundraiser for the club. In the past, the president of the club was not responsible for this project, but because George had become the go-to guy in the club, he was given the responsibility.

Now you can imagine, a task like this takes a great deal of work. George was not the type of person to delegate responsibility because, in the past, he had been "burned." Of course, there is no way he could do all the work himself. He got volunteers to do some of the physical work and to work the event itself. But George took on the responsibility of all of the organizing, all of the phone calling, all of the publicity, all of the ... well, you get the idea.

The event turned out quite well. Many participants complimented George on being the director of a very successful triathlon. Yet when George looked behind him, he did not feel successful. He was exhausted, and he knew that he had damaged relationships with some of the club members. He had snapped at his wife on numerous occasions simply because he was over-tired. He felt over-worked and under-appreciated. He realized that there was no way he could receive enough appreciation to "pay" for what he had gone through.

In addition, George's doctor snarled at him for letting his blood pressure go up. He was not able to exercise as he was used to doing, so he gained weight and felt lousy. He stayed up late trying to get work for the triathlon done as well as trying to catch up on his own business assignments. When he did get to bed, he could not get to sleep easily. And when he did sleep, he dreamt about the triathlon.

Bottom line, even though the event was a success, George felt like a failure and never wanted to organize the triathlon again. George felt like he had given away a big chunk of his life.

Sound familiar? The kinds of interactions, decisions and issues George faced are similar to what we see you facing on a daily basis. Unfortunately, we also see the same kinds of results George experienced in you as well time and time again. Whether you are a manager of a department, a job captain or a project manager, we know from experience, the "George Syndrome" is all too common in America!

So, when the "George Syndrome" is so pervasive and so emotionally draining, why should you delegate at all? It is quite simple. If you delegate effectively, you can eliminate the personal cost of overwork that George experienced. This means that you get your life back. Your family gets to see more of you. Your relationships with others improve. Your health and well-being take a decided turn for the better.

Fortunately, George has learned the secrets of successful, hassle-free delegation. He still organizes the triathlon, but it is much easier for him now because he knows he cannot do it all himself. He relies on others to do much of the organizational work. And, because he knows those secrets of successful delegation, he knows they will get the job done ... and they do.

BUILDING BETTER RELATIONSHIPS

In the discussion above, we mentioned that when you are able to delegate effectively, your relationships with others improve. There is little mystery behind this if you think about it. When you delegate responsibility properly, you get the person who accepts the delegation (team member) personally involved in the process. If she is successful—and given your coaching and guidance she will be—her sense of accomplishment increases, and she feels good about herself and what she has done. There are a number of reasons for this sense of accomplishment and benefits that accrue due to successful delegation.

1. People rise to the occasion when properly informed and trained.

When given the resources, the people in business with you or in organizations you belong to enjoy challenges. They will rise to the occasion when given challenges. There is an important caveat here, though. They will do so when they have been given—and know they have been given—all of the resources they will need to accomplish this. This is the core of effective, hassle-free delegation, and we will get to this later in the book.

20

2. People learn from the tasks they do when they have responsibility delegated to them.

People invariably learn new skills, procedures, facts, or ideas when they are given a challenge through the delegation process. But even if everything in the project is "old hat" to them, they still will be able to hone skills and learn new ways of doing things. If nothing else, they will have learned the power of effective delegation and how it should be done properly. They will walk away with greater respect and understanding of the process so that they can use it in the future. No one finishes a properly delegated task without learning something new.

3. People gain ownership of the project or task when they have a part in it.

Ownership of a project is an obvious benefit of delegating responsibility, but it is one that is frequently overlooked. When people work on a project and have been given the tools they need to succeed, they have a stake in it.

For example, let us say your boss has charged you with being responsible for getting a monthly division newsletter out. She has made it clear that she does not expect you to do it yourself. She just wants it done. So you approach someone in your division whom you know or sense has graphic and writing skills. You give him clear directions and provide him with the time, tools, and training to accomplish the task. Mark my words, the first time the newsletter is delivered throughout your division, your editor will be eager to see how it is received. You will notice him saying things such as "In *my* next issue, I'll ... " At this point you know that he has taken ownership of this project. This result of effective delegation is in itself a good thing, but there is an additional effect that is even more beneficial to all concerned.

4. People buy-in to the company or organization.

By giving someone responsibility for a project or task along with the necessary resources to complete it properly and well, you have increased their "buy-in" or stake in the organization they are working for.

21

In the example of the editor of the newsletter, this man will take ownership of the project and will work to make sure it is done well because its success is his success. He now has a "product" that is a part of the organization, a product that ties him to that organization. Now of course, there are other activities and consequences necessary to maintain and strengthen that tie (which we will discuss later in the book), but the seed has been planted. You now have an associate who has a potentially very strong stake in your organization.

5. When people have been given responsibility, they are able to share in the limelight.

This is another obvious result of successful delegation. Our fictitious editor is not the only one accidentally referring to the newsletter as "his." Other people in the company will also call it "his newsletter." Let's say one of them has an idea for an issue. She is likely to approach the editor and say, "I have an idea for *your* newsletter." If he is working in an organization that exhibits good management skills, he will be acknowledged by those higher up for his efforts.

When looking at the finished product (be it a newsletter, a triathlon, or any delegated project), the delegatee can proudly state, "I did that!"

The concept of True Teamwork suggests we want to give recognition and show appreciation to all members of the team. Each team member needs to understand he or she cannot do anything alone, and so shouldn't take all the credit alone. What we are talking about here is the sense of ownership that naturally goes along with a successful delegation.

22

6. People's self-respect will increase.

There is not a person alive who does not like to receive accolades for her accomplishments. This is simply a part of human nature. One of the beautiful parts about effective delegation is that everybody involved feels this sense of accomplishment and with it a rising sense of self-worth and self-respect. So, one of the powerful effects of delegation when done properly is that you will be working among people who want to work with you ... who feel committed to your organization ... and who demonstrate a high degree of self-confidence and self-worth when they are working for you.

What more could you want from successful delegation?

HOW ABOUT 60 TO 1 SUPER-LEVERAGE POWER?

Let's go back to the newsletter that your boss asked you to get started for your division. Recall that he specifically said that you did not have to do it yourself. However, you know this is a pet project of your boss, and you absolutely do not want it messed up. You do what you have always done in situations such as this: You decide to do it yourself.

Now you are saddled with a project that initially could take twenty hours or more as you struggle with software, layout, getting stories, and actually producing and distributing the thing. And once you have gone through the difficult break-in time, you are still looking at producing the newsletter every month, having to commit between two and five hours of work.

On the other hand, how long would it take you to give clearly delegated responsibility for this project to someone who would enjoy doing it? Probably not much more than twenty to thirty minutes. When you do the math, you are looking at leveraging your time 60 to 1 (20 minutes versus 20 hours or more).

This is *powerful* <u>leverage</u>. However, successful delegation does not stop at leveraging your time. Effective delegation can save money as well as wasted effort. A large United States manufacturing corporation with which the Truby Achievement Center worked provides a telling example of this leverage. (The firm must for legal reasons remain unnamed.

This firm was under an Environmental Protection Agency consent decree to move 750,000 cubic yards of potentially contaminated sediment out of a river bed. This massive project involved dredging, water treatment, and landfill at a projected cost of over $35 million. This is pure cost with no chance for profit from the expenditure. This is a cost that the firm badly wanted to contain.

As you might expect, the firm had to hire quite a few sub-contractors to do this project, there not being any one company large enough with all the expertise to manage the entire project. This is a system ripe for disaster. With so many subcontractors and groups working, the opportunity for inefficiency and cost overruns is enormous.

In order to mitigate this situation, it was necessary to form the various disparate groups into teams that could work effectively and efficiently together. The Truby Achievement Center was called in to work with this firm and its subcontractors to help organize these teams and to minimize problems within them and to maximize their efficiency.

A major part of our work was to establish cohesive teams composed of the different subcontractors and representatives from the firm. Then we undertook to teach these team leaders the same process of delegation that you are learning in this book.

Before finding an unexpected instability in the banks of the river, this project had saved a projected $2 to $3 million dollars through using this process. (There still should be significant savings as the team efficiently deals with this change in the project's parameters). This financial benefit, too, is significant leverage resulting from improved group/corporate practices and successful delegation techniques we taught them.

24

LACK OF DELEGATION COULD BE CAUSING INVERSE LEVERAGE IN YOUR LIFE

While delegation has powerful leverage effectiveness, failure to delegate has its own leverage. But this time, the leverage power is working against you to the detriment of you and your life. This is what we call <u>inverse leverage</u>. We have already discussed how trying to do it all yourself will take a toll on your career, your relationships, and your life. Ask yourself now, what in your life is not getting done because you cannot delegate responsibility?

The things in your life that need to be done but are not getting done have a powerful inverse leverage on your life. The dinners missed at home, the rushed projects at work, the "adequately" finished activities in your social world, the excess stress in your life will—without a doubt—come back to bite you. When they do, the damage that is done takes longer and more work to repair than if you attended to them properly in the first place.

Using the example of the large firm we just discussed, if the teams did not receive the training in effective delegation or did not implement it, do you think there would have been a financial savings? Certainly not. You know the euphemism that is used in cases such as this: cost overrun. What it really is, is throwing money down the toilet. Would you expect that the cost overrun in this case to be the amount that the firm saved? Not on your life. You and we both know that in situations like this, the money tossed down the toilet would be far greater than the amount that might have been saved.

So it is with your life. The long-term cost of not delegating responsibility effectively is tremendous … and often times *cannot* be repaid.

IT'S YOUR CHOICE: A HARMONIOUS ORCHESTRA … 25
OR DISCORDANT, SOUR NOTES

We challenge you to name me a famous one-man band. Then we challenge you to name a famous jazz orchestra.

We are willing to bet you came up blank on the first challenge. One-man bands are novelties at best, but they seldom, if ever, produce harmonious music. But we just as willing to bet that you could come up with several names of famous jazz orchestras: Benny Goodman, Count Basie and Duke Ellington are three obvious ones.

Look at Duke Ellington. He is an excellent example of successful delegation. He was always *clearly* the leader of his orchestra, but he allowed his musicians freedom to express themselves. Some of his most famous music—Take the A Train, the orchestra's theme song—were composed by his musicians not him. (Billy Strayhorn in this case).

Ellington taught and directed his orchestra and produced beautiful music as a result. He understood well that no one person can play all of the instruments and still come up with harmonious music. While this seems obvious when talking about an orchestra, this is not an easy lesson for many of us to learn when it applies to our own personal, social or professional lives. It is a difficult lesson, but it is an important one.

To Recap What You Have Learned In This Chapter:

There are quite a few powerful reasons for delegating, but they can all be grouped into the following areas:

- improved personal, social, and professional effectiveness,
- improved personal, social, and business relationships,
- powerful leverage of time (up to 6000%),
- powerful leverage of money, and
- powerful leverage of effort.

Now it is time to start learning the secrets of hassle-free delegation. In our next six chapters, you will learn the five steps that will allow you get other people to work effectively and efficiently for everyone's benefit.

CHAPTER 3
A ROAD MAP FOR EFFECTIVE DELEGATION

In this chapter you will learn:

- The five steps of effective delegation
  1. Delegate accountability;
  2. Assess progress;
  3. Determine reasons for lack of success (if necessary);
  4. Re-initiate process (if necessary);
  5. Reward appropriately;
- The importance in getting "ownership" of the project or task;
- How to get ownership;
- How family values differ from family dynamics in the delegation process and the importance of relentless accountability.

Before beginning on a trip of discovery as we are about to do, it is best if we look at a road map first. That is this chapter's purpose. The five steps for effective delegation are easy to understand, but as you will see shortly, the steps are not linear.

If you want to delegate responsibility effectively, you must have a feedback system built in so that you know your delegation is actually working. This feedback loop aspect makes the road map look a bit complicated, but it is not. In fact, the entire system is extremely simple and easy to apply and can be accomplished in a matter of minutes on simpler projects with all the benefits of leverage we talked about earlier.

27

SUCCESSFUL DELEGATION SYSTEM

STEP 1

Delegate Accountability

Include Responsibility and Authority

28

STEP 2

ASSESS PROGRESS

STEP 2

ASSESS PROGRESS

STEP 4

RE-INITIATE PROCESS

Limited or no follow-through

Successful follow-through

DETERMINE CAUSES **STEP 3**

STEP 5

REWARD APPROPRIATELY

Remediate

Continued lack of follow-through

Termination from the *team*

Everyone involved reaps the benefits of effective delegation.

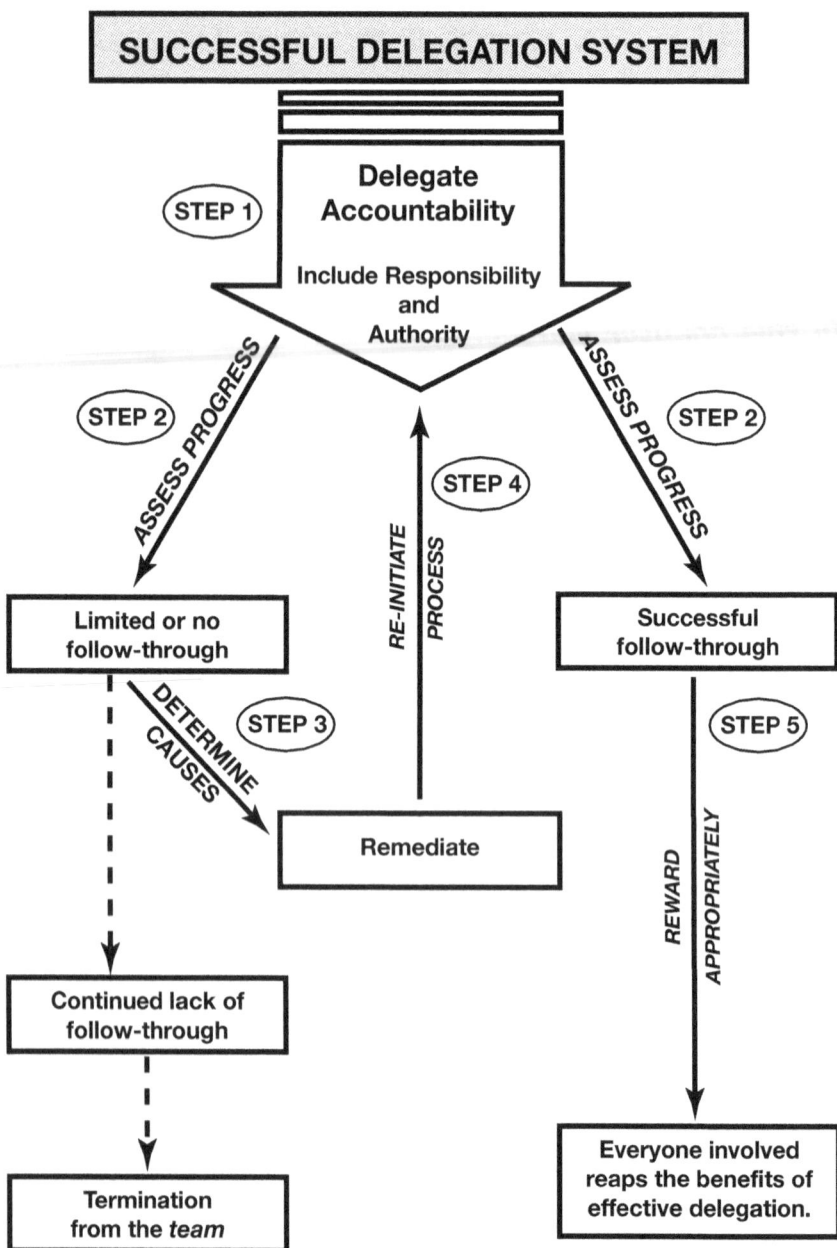

Figure 3.1 Our road map for effective delegation

In this chapter, we will look at this road map on a large scale for quick understanding. In subsequent chapters, we will present detailed discussions of each step. If these steps seem a bit unclear as to their implementation in this chapter, I assure you, they will become clear in the chapters devoted to them. That said, let us take a moment to look at the road map of where we are going in Figure 3.1.

As you can see, the diagram is *not* linear. On the left side of the diagram, steps 2, 3 and 4 form the feedback loop we mentioned. You will notice that another characteristic of this diagram is that there are two "Step 2's" depending on the outcome of your evaluation of the process.

Let's now look at the steps along the way in somewhat greater detail.

STEP 1: Delegate Accountability

The obvious first step in delegation would be to actually do it, to tell the person to whom you are delegating the task and what you hope to get from him. However, before you even get to that stage, you need to be clear yourself what you are asking him to do and how you will give him all the support he needs to accomplish the task. In Chapter 4, we go into the details of how to get clear on this yourself and how to provide the support to the person.

For starters, let us clarify the expression "delegate *accountability*." You will notice that throughout much of this book we use the expressions "responsibility," "authority," and "accountability" interchangeably. These expressions are *not* equivalent, but they are all so tightly interwoven into the entire process that they can be used almost interchangeably. Effective delegation encompasses delegating all three factors, as you shall see in the next chapter.

You cannot expect people to accept delegated tasks and to accomplish them competently if you do not give them the sense that they are responsible for the tasks' completion. Likewise, you cannot expect the tasks to be done well unless there is some structure of accountability, so that the people delegated to know that they have to accomplish the task to some set of standards.

These two aspects of delegation are necessary, but they are not sufficient. People need to feel they have the authority necessary to accomplish all parts of the tasks that have been delegated. Without that authority, it is unreasonable for them to be expected to accomplish the tasks. You will learn more about this in the next chapter as well.

30

STEP 2: ASSESS PROGRESS

All too often, when people delegate tasks to others, they fail to do a very important—and simple—part of the process. That is, they fail to assess progress and follow-through until it is too late. Perhaps you have fallen into this trap.

Our map splits into two parts at this part of the road map, Step 2. The right side indicates that the evaluation has shown that the tasks delegated have been accomplished with appropriate follow-through. This is the hoped for outcome every time we delegate tasks, but as we discussed previously, it is not the common experience most of us have.

So, in Chapter 5, we will spend a significant amount of time discussing how to assess progress toward completion of the delegated tasks as well as ways to remediate problems when there is little or no follow-through. Suffice it to say, if you do not take the time to make this evaluation during and at the end of the delegation process, you will always fall into the trap of "it wasn't done right, completely or on time."

STEP 3: DETERMINE CAUSES AND REMEDIATE

Let's go back to the story of our friend George and the triathlon. One of the tasks he had delegated (unsuccessfully) to another member of the team, Dan—a friend of his as well as a member of the club—was to get highway safety signs for use on the bike and run routes. The event takes place on the Sunday of Labor Day weekend, and the signs *had* to be picked up by noon on Thursday. They were not. No signs; no race.

George panicked momentarily then thought of a reasonable alternative. Because of the timing of the event, George did not have an opportunity to do anything other than get signs from another source. Afterward he swore he would *never* depend on Dan to help him again.

However, after learning our process of effective delegation, George was willing to find out what went wrong in this instance.

George was surprised that a good number of the reasons that his efforts at delegation failed were because of his own lack of understanding of how to make the process work. He realized that Dan did not have the sense of urgency about the matter that George did. George had passed on the information that the items needed to be picked up by noon on Thursday, but he had not passed on the urgency of the deadline. Dan thought he would be able to pick them up on Friday when he missed the Thursday deadline.

There were other problems in this fairly typical delegation process that had to do with Dan and his lack of a strong sense of commitment. But once George had determined the causes of the problems, he was ready to go on to the next part of the process, remediating the problems.

In a follow-up meeting with Dan, they were able to discuss the problems that had happened. Working together using the processes we discuss in Chapter 5, the men were able to find reasonable solutions to the problems. George decided to give his friend another chance for the next year's triathlon. But he did not do so in the same way. Instead, he took the fourth step in our process.

STEP 4: RE-INITIATE THE PROCESS

Once George and Dan understood the source and nature of the problems, it was easy for them to agree to try again. They both did so with a greater understanding of their individual responsibilities in the process and how to make it work better. And they both did so after an informal re-negotiation of what was expected of both of them.

George is glad he trusted his friend. The next year, Dan did his delegated task on time and completely, and he went beyond what was expected of him. George did not let the delegation process falter there, however. He went on to the fifth and final step.

STEP 5: REWARD THE EFFORTS OF OTHERS

Directing a triathlon, even a small one, can be an overwhelmingly complex and stressful activity, even when aspects of it are delegated properly. Once the event is over, it is all too easy for the person in charge to go home, flop down on the couch, pick up a tall cool one, and try to put the event out of his mind.

This is a mistake. Regardless of the type of task that has been delegated—from the simplest to the most complex—people delegated responsibility *have* to be acknowledged and rewarded in some way or another. We will discuss this in detail in Chapter 6, but suffice it to say right now, that the reward does *not* have to have any extrinsic value.

The team member receives numerous benefits from the process that come simply as a result of having gone through it successfully. This said, though, acknowledgement of a "job well done" will go a long way to ensuring that you continue to be an effective delegater.

Ownership

If you want your efforts at delegating to be successful, you absolutely must infuse a sense of ownership of the project or product into the person to whom you are delegating. The issue of ownership in the project runs parallel to the entire process, so it is best described here as opposed to in any particular stage of the delegation process. Ownership is a sense of purpose, responsibility, and authority a person delegated a task feels when they fully accept it as *their* task to accomplish. As mentioned in Chapter 2, one of the effects of successful delegation is that the person gets a sense of buy-in with the organization for which they are working.

33

This buy-in is a direct reaction to their ownership of the project that takes place prior to it being completed. In fact, if Step 1 is done correctly, ownership begins there. Because team members have claimed ownership of the project, that ownership connects them in powerful ways to the organization. If the person to whom you are delegating the task does not feel ownership in the project, the delegation will be nothing more than a chore.

HOW TO CREATE OWNERSHIP

Creating ownership in a project being delegated is not much different than securing ownership in life. For simplicity sake, then, we will look at what changes simple possession of an automobile into a sense of ownership.

There are three basic factors that cause people to feel as if they own something. These are investment, freedom, and reward.

Investment

For us to feel that we truly own something, we must have a sense of <u>investment</u> in it. This can be an investment of money or time, but the investment must be there.

Let's imagine for a moment that Michael Anthony from the "Millionaire" visits you. (If you are too young to remember this great 60s television program, it involved Michael Anthony giving away a tax-free check for $1,000,000 every week). Instead of your receiving a check however, you are in a second tier of gift recipients who receive a free car. Michael Anthony stands at the door and hands you the keys to a brand new Mercedes-Benz SL500.

As you look out in your driveway, your mouth waters as you look at your new, 300 horsepower, V-8, silver, streamlined convertible. You can hardly contain yourself as you rush to your new car. You open the door, and you are not greeted by the "new car smell." Instead, the scent of soft leather fills your nose.

You slip behind the wheel as Michael Anthony stands beside you, gently encouraging you to try it out. As you slip the key in the ignition several feelings overtake you: excitement, joy, confusion.

Confusion? Of course. As you are about to drive "your" new car, you feel that something is not quite right. You know it is yours. Michael Anthony has given you the keys and the pink slip on it. But it just does not feel quite right. As you drive off, it feels as if you are test-driving the Benz straight from the showroom floor. You feel as if you will be asked for the keys back at any moment.

You tell yourself that this strange feeling will pass, after all it isn't everyday that someone gives you a $90,000 automobile. But the feeling never really passes entirely. You keep your fancy car in the garage except for the most special occasions and continue driving your Hyundai Excel to work and the store. You tell yourself and others it's because you want to keep it in tip-top shape.

The reality is you just do not feel comfortable calling it yours. The reason is you have not made any real investment in it and psychologically we need to make some kind of investment, either time or money, in something to really *feel* it is ours. In this case, you have not done anything to really make it yours. Consequently, you do not feel like you own it.

Alternatively, instead of squirreling the Mercedes-Benz away in your garage, you might feel that lack of real ownership gives you the freedom to drive recklessly in it, to push it up to the 110 m.p.h. it is easily capable of doing. After all, if you wreck it, or drop the transmission, or otherwise mistreat it, you didn't pay anything for it so there is no big loss. This is known in the business as the "rental car syndrome."

We have all heard of kids who received an expensive car from their parents who promptly left it in a heap of steel and rubber. The same phenomenon is at work with people whose lives get "ruined" by winning the lotto.

35

Let us say, though, that when Michael Anthony hands you the keys and the pink slip, he tells you there is just one small catch. You must use the car one day a week for one year to take a child from the local orphanage to the doctor's office. (Come on; bear with us. This was 60s television).

Now when you first start driving the little boy to the doctor, you may still feel like you do not really own the car. But that feeling will soon fade as you justify your ownership by the good deed you are performing.

Alternatively, after you have spent sufficient time with your gift, that time becomes the investment that can instill ownership. Either spending time with something that has been given you or exchanging something of value for it begins to give a sense of ownership.

Investment in a project or task also plays a major role in creating ownership in the delegation process. The person you are delegating to will feel a greater sense of ownership if he is allowed to invest in the project. Now, of course he will invest his time (or not) while he is working on the task, but investment in this case must go beyond that. You increase his sense of ownership of the project by having him understand the importance of his participation. You will get that investment by acknowledging it ahead of time and at various stages along the way.

One of the best ways to secure investment in a project you are delegating is to acknowledge the person's investment. It is a simple part of the process, but it is one that is often times overlooked. This acknowledgment can be as simple as a sentence or two recognizing how important the person's efforts are and how much they are appreciated. It can also be a simple "thank you" for the person choosing to work and exercise their talents and skills in your team, for investing their time in this organization. In short, *acknowledging* a person's investment of time and talent will create an awareness of the investment in them.

36   Be sincere when you do this. If you truly feel appreciation for the person's efforts, she will sense it in you. For this reason, it is important for you to understand the degree of personal investment the task requires. When done properly, this type of acknowledgment can go a long, long way to securing the investment necessary to create ownership in a project.

Freedom

Imagine for a moment that as Michael Anthony hands you the keys and the pink slip to the Mercedes-Benz SL500, he tells you that you must use the car *only* to take the boy in the orphanage to the doctor's. Would you feel any sense of ownership at all?

Of course not. You would feel as if you were an unpaid chauffeur. The only benefit you derive from this "gift" is being seen in town every Friday in a fancy car that is not yours. Other than that, the car might as well be sitting in the dealer's showroom. Imagine what you would feel like when your friends ask you for a ride in your new car. It would be hard to explain the restriction and still call the car your own.

In order to create ownership of a project or a product, freedom to act with it must also be given. Now this does not mean absolute freedom. In both cases there have to be parameters within which the person can operate. But pull the reins too tight, and the person to whom you are delegating will feel like a child being directed and will not feel ownership of the project.

The parameters within which you allow freedom depend, of course, on the project (or object). If you were to give a teenage boy an automobile, you might secure investment from him by having him pay for the insurance or do errands with it as a condition of his keeping the car.

The freedom you give him might be within the parameters of when he can drive (not after eight on school nights), where he can drive (within county lines), and how he can drive (seat belts, within speed limit, no alcohol). Other than those parameters, your son is free to use the car as he wishes.

The same holds true for projects you delegate and the people you delegate them to. The second time our friend George delegated the road sign job to Dan, he gave him freedom to collect the signs for the triathlon whenever he wanted to except within the parameters established by the hours the county road department was open (not on Fridays, remember?) and not more than a week in advance.

Dan understood he could do it at his convenience within those parameters. The first time, however, the time where Dan had not followed through, George had told Dan that he needed to pick up the signs on Thursday before noon. Dan did not have the freedom he needed to complete the task. Consequently, he did not get ownership of the project and did not follow through.

Reward

If there is no <u>reward</u>, there is no ownership. Plain and simple. Now, we usually think of reward as coming at the end of a project in the form of a celebration, payment, recognition, or the like. The type of reward that helps create ownership does not necessarily have to be this type of reward. In fact, it often is not. Often, it is something intrinsic in the project or object of which we want to create ownership.

37

Let's take a negative example to start. In this scenario, Michael Anthony rings your doorbell and gives you the same elegant speech about how a certain benefactor who wishes to remain anonymous has given you full possession of a car for you to use as you please. The only hitch is the same one as before. You must drive a little boy from the orphanage to the doctor one day a week.

You have investment (your time taking the boy to the doctor). You have freedom. Do you now have ownership?

You look outside and sitting in your driveway—instead of a gleaming silver Mercedes-Benz SL500—is a rusted out, banged up 1972 Ford Pinto with Firestone 500 tires. Do you now have ownership?

No way! You would tell Michael Anthony to take his hunk of junk off your property and not return. Ownership would not be created in this case simply because you did not want ownership. In this case owning the banged up Pinto has no <u>intrinsic</u> reward value.

However, if Michael Anthony gently led you by the arm and let you look inside the beaten-up Ford, and pointed out piles of $100 bills on the back seat, you might change your mind about the old jalopy. You would want ownership; there is something in this case that makes the gift valuable.

So it is with delegated responsibility. The person you are delegating to must sense that there is some intrinsic or <u>extrinsic</u> payoff for her. This reward can be a typical reward at the end of the project such as a fair wage, profit sharing, cash bonus, and press coverage. Or it can be something inherent in the project.

One of the ways George solved the problem with his friend Dan was to explain in detail what needed to be done and when it need to be accomplished. He gave Dan the freedom to do it within the parameters established by the county roads department. He also explained the importance of this task, something he had not done before. George explained how important the signs were in keeping the runners and bicyclists safe while on the roads and how important the fundraiser was to the clubs local community projects. He had Dan imagine high school students receiving a $1,000 scholarship from the club or 3rd graders receiving free dictionaries of their very own.

By giving these details, George was able to create ownership in the project because Dan got intrinsic rewards from knowing that he was responsible for an important part of an important event. George solidified that ownership by telling Dan that the club would be running an ad in the local paper thanking all the volunteers by name. George was careful not to tell Dan all this in a way that would make Dan feel bad about his previous year's lack of follow-through. He told his friend in such a way that Dan could feel good about his participation—one of the best rewards anyone can have when delegated a project.

FOUR CRITICAL COMPONENTS THAT HELP CREATE OWNERSHIP

We have found that there are four components in creating ownership that are critical to the success of the three-step process. These are giving purpose and context and instilling inspiration and motivation. While these four components can be looked at individually, they are so closely intertwined that it is in practice almost impossible to separate them.

The first piece of the process is "giving purpose and context." Purpose is the "why" for the "what," in other words, the reason you are asking a person to do a task.

Context is how the project or task fits into the bigger picture of your organization. Giving purpose and context (if indeed you have given true purpose and context—to be explained shortly) *always* increases inspiration and motivation to do the job. By doing so, you help the person develop her own sense of ownership.

Let's look at some details of this part of the process of instilling ownership ... and let's do so in the context of your being assigned a task.

When your boss tells you to do something it still may be just a task ... you may be *motivated* to do it to keep your job. Continued employment is a strong motivator, after all. But simply wanting to keep your job may not be much of a stimulus to make you feel inspired to do the task with any degree of a sense of ownership. In other words, you still may not have any *inspiration*. In essence, the boss's simply telling you what to do may or may not reap the results of motivation and/or inspiration. The chances of doing so are increased if you are given the purpose and context of the task.

40

Our take is this: When you give purpose and context clearly and effectively, you *always* reap some degree of inspiration and motivation.

One important ingredient regarding purpose and context is to give it in the language and perspective of the person being delegated to, *not* in the context of the organization.

Take, for example, the situation of highly utilized employees. From the organization's perspective, the purpose and context would be this: Purpose—to have every resource in the organization used to the maximum to reap the greatest return. Context—how employees' work fits into the rest of the operations of the organization.

To the employees, the purpose and context are significantly different. They would be this: Purpose—to have their talents and abilities utilized and maximized, to maintain their place in the organization, to do complete assigned tasks or projects as preparation or training for larger tasks or roles in the organization. Context – how the employees' contributions on particular tasks or projects contribute to the success of their teams or the organization as a whole.

The following example illustrates these points. Let us say that you work on the 20th floor of a high rise building in a city close to the mountains. Your boss comes to you and hands you a box. He tells you, "Take this box down to the curb. A trucking company will pick it up from you in about fifteen minutes."

Your motivation is at this stage simply that your boss has given you a direction. Due to the power difference inherent in that relationship, this motivation is sufficient for you to perform the task. But have you yet taken ownership of it? Probably not. The task is just something your boss requires you to do. You may decide to take the box, stop at the employee cafeteria for a cup of coffee along the way, and make it down to the curb with a minute or two to spare.

41

Your boss continues talking to you. He gives a <u>context</u> that gives you more information about the task. He tells you that the box contains high power explosives.

Now, this context may indicate a great deal about how you complete the task. For starters, you may feel that fifteen minutes are not enough for you to complete the task. You may decide that you need to use the freight elevator instead of the main one. And that stop for a cup of coffee is definitely out.

By adding context to the instructions, your boss has given you another piece of the puzzle, a piece that can make your ownership of the task more solid. He is entrusting you with a dangerous task.

By giving you that context, you may decide to decline the task, which may seem like a negative, but it is far from being so. After all, when you are delegating a task, you want to be sure the person you are delegating to will perform the task in its context. If he is not willing to do so, you should know up front so you can find another person for the task.

So back to your boss telling you about your taking this package of high explosives down to the curb. He has given you motivation and inspiration (his assigning you the task). He has provided context for you (high explosives). He now gives you the final piece of important information.

There has been a landslide in the mountains and it has trapped a busload of children. No one is hurt, but the kids need to be rescued as quickly as possible. Given this final piece of the puzzle—the <u>purpose</u> behind the task —you now can decide if this is a project for which you want to claim ownership.

You now have the choice of making an investment in the project. Your investment will be your effort. Your boss has given you freedom to do it in any safe manner possible within the parameter of having to accomplish it within fifteen minutes. And you have a two-part reward. He tells you that when the press calls for the story, he will be sure that you get credit for your contribution. But the biggest reward for you is that you know a busload of young children is safe and on their way home because of your effort.

You are now motivated … and because of this have taken personal ownership of a project that just moments before was little more than just a task to be done.

FAMILY VALUES … NOT FAMILY DYNAMICS

Often you will hear it said about an organization, "we are just one big family here." This has a nice ring to it, but in fact, organizations and successful teams should not be entirely like families, at least in the complete sense of the way families frequently interact with their members. It is important, then, that when you delegate responsibility as part of a team, you know what part of "family" needs to be encouraged and what part needs to be discarded.

The part of "family" to keep in the delegation process—or in any successful group dynamics—is the part that celebrates the <u>family values</u> of love, trust, support, and caring. There is not a well functioning organization in existence that does not have a strong commitment to these values. If you bring these values into the delegation process, the process, the outcomes, and all the people involved will benefit greatly.

However, when delegating authority, we want to keep <u>family dynamics</u> out of the process. While family values help encourage and promote success, typical family dynamics limit it.

Typically, family dynamics exhibit a **lack of <u>open communication</u>**. Secrets are a big part of family dynamics. Parents keep things hidden from the children; children keep things hidden from the parents.

43

On the other hand, open communication is vitally important in delegation as it is in successful high performing teams. The Blue Angels are a clear example of how critical open communication can be. In this team, every member has a particular role he must fill. Each member must look to the leader and follow his lead. However, a constant flow of information between all the members of the team keeps all of them safe.

Open communication may not have the obvious dramatic impact in business and delegation that it does for the Blue Angels, but it remains a crucial part of the picture. When delegating a task to another person, you need her to feel free to communicate with you on all aspects of the project, good and bad. Likewise, she needs to be given as much information as possible so that she can complete the task efficiently and effectively.

Frequently within families there is a **lack of <u>accountability</u>**. Johnny may be cajoled and nagged to make his bed, but if he does not do so, often there is no real price to pay. Children are seldom now "sent to bed without their supper." (In fact, this type of accountability has always been more celebrated in the breech than in the observance to use William Shakespeare's words).

Children who are not consistently accountable are simply "put up with" until they leave the nest. Recognize that? Often unaccountable team members are put up with while others hope they will eventually leave. Often they are even moved around in the organization—sometimes even promoted—while being put up with, much to the eventual detriment of the organization.

Strong, well functioning businesses honor accountability. People who do well are promoted. People who perform poorly are moved around until an appropriate spot is found where they can do well. If no such place is found, they are terminated.

44

This may not seem humane, but ultimately is. All organizations need to function effectively in order to be successful or make a profit. Ones that are overly "gracious" with their employees, allowing incompetence to go on unchecked, will ultimately fail. A failed business does no one any good: not the competent employees or the incompetent ones. Lack of accountability is the death knell of business.

Graciousness can keep you from greatness.

So it is with delegation. Accountability is crucial to successful delegation. All parties to the delegation need to have clear standards by which they are evaluated or assessed. The people involved need to know what needs to be done, who needs to do it, and when the task needs to be accomplished. An expression that clarifies these standards is this (and you will hear this again several times in the next few chapters:

What? By Whom? By When?
The "mantra" of clear accountability.

In families, there is usually a lack of <u>shared ownership</u> of the process of: raising the family. Everyone—the family, neighbors, the community, and society in general—considers parents to be responsible for the success or failure of the family unit. However, when problems arise or persist, all members of the family tend to blame one another.

So Melissa is failing in school. Mom says, "If only she would study harder." Dad says, "If only my wife would help her with her homework." Brother says, "If only she weren't such a dweeb." Melissa says, "if only they would stop fighting I would feel like doing better in school."

Blame is a sign of family dynamics at work wherever it occurs. It is an indicator to you that your group, organization, or business is mired in family dynamics ... dynamics that will keep your organization from greatness ... and dynamics that can prevent effective delegation of responsibility.

When there is lack of shared ownership, there is a disparate imbalance in power. The supervisor or boss (parent) tells people what to do, the implicit "why" being because "I told you so." When people are treated this way, they feel like children.

Ownership helps people grow up. When a person feels they have ownership of a project—and with that ownership responsibility for its successful completion—they then feel they have stepped out of the morass of family dynamics. They are ready to take full responsibility for what they have been delegated.

In the next chapter, we will go back to the very first step in our delegation system and discuss it in greater detail. You will notice that this step and each subsequent step are more detailed than we have presented in the initial large-scale road map in this chapter.

To Recap What You Have Learned In This Chapter:

Delegation of responsibility is an easy process that can be successfully accomplished when you pay attention to the steps and parameters surrounding it.

- The five steps of effective delegation are:
  1. Delegate Accountability;
  2. Assess progress and follow-through;
  3. Determine reasons for lack of success (if necessary) and remediate them;
  4. Re-initiate process (if necessary);
  5. Reward appropriately.
- "Ownership" of a project is necessary for its successful completion.
- You create ownership through:
  - Supporting investment in the project and acknowledging that investment;
  - Allowing freedom within specified parameters;
  - Rewarding participation extrinsically and intrinsically.
- The important components in creating ownership (PCIM) are:
  - Purpose;
  - Context;
  - Inspiration
  - Motivation.
- Family values are to be encouraged in the delegation process. Family dynamics are to be discarded.
- Characteristics of family dynamics and their desired counterparts are:
  - Lack of open communication/open communication;
  - Lack of accountability/accountability;
  - Lack of shared ownership/shared ownership.
- Blame is a sign of family dynamics.
- Ownership allows people to grow up.

CHAPTER 4

STEP 1: INITIATING THE DELEGATION PROCESS

In this chapter you will learn:

- What you need to do before you "officially" start the process
- How to create a contract of expectations:
  - What?
  - By whom?
  - By when?
- The importance of purpose and context in the process;
- How to clarify cause and effect results;
- The necessity of providing resources for successful completion of the project;
- How to incorporate monitoring/measuring systems.

47

The obvious first step in delegating a task is to tell the person what needs to be done. And it is ... almost. If you look at Figure 4.1 on the next page—a blown-up section of Step 1 of our Road Map to Effective Delegation—you will see that there are six components involved, but that we have numbered them from 0 to 5 instead of from 1 to 6.

We did this intentionally. We wanted to emphasize the importance of the first component and to indicate to you that it really *has* to come before you do any of the other components of this step.

In order for the delegation to go smoothly and effectively, *you* must have clarity yourself on what you need to do specifically to structure the delegation for maximum effectiveness. This seems to be an evident part of delegation process that you will prepare for prior to going into the actual delegation process. This is a quite simple concept; you do your "homework" ahead of time. However, it is a concept we all too often forget when going into this process.

The primary reason that many people fail to prepare ahead of time for the actual act of delegating a task to another person is that del-egaters often do not have a clear understanding of what they should be doing at the initial contact other than assigning a task. For this reason, we will go through components 1 through 5 first and then return to the necessary prelude.

**SUCCESSFUL DELEGATION SYSTEM
Step 1**

**Delegate
Accountability**

Include Responsibility
and
Authority

0. Research thoroughly the details of components 1-5 for the task or project being delegated.
1. Create contract of expectations:
    a. What? Clarify the end product.
    b. By whom? Include peripheral people; identify the accountability leader.
    c. By when? Be specific.
2. Provide purpose and context.
3. Clarify cause and effect results.
4. Determine and provide resources necessary for effective completion
5. Determine monitoring/measuring system, especially for longer time-lines.

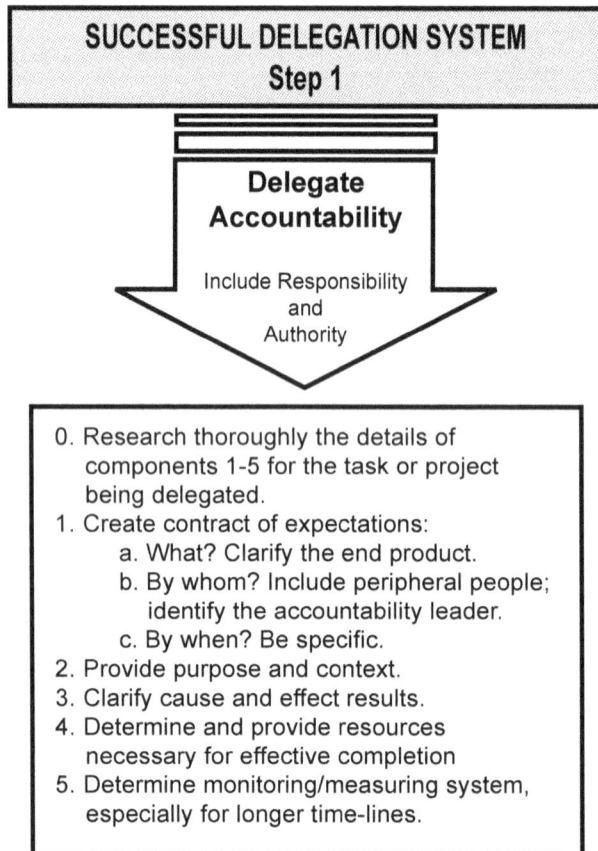

Figure 4.1 Successful delegation: Step 1

RESPONSIBILITY, AUTHORITY, AND ACCOUNTABILITY: THREE PIECES COMPLETING THE DELEGATION PUZZLE

Earlier in this book we said that we would use the expressions delegating accountability, delegating responsibility, and delegating authority almost interchangeably. It is possible to do so because each of these three factors provides an absolutely necessary part of the delegation process, but no one of them is sufficient in itself. They are like three interlocking pieces of a puzzle as we see in Figure 4.2

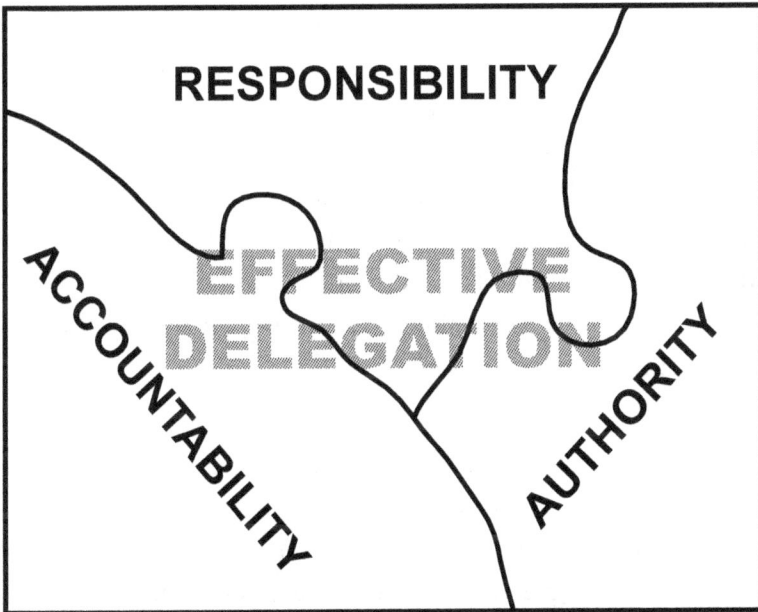

Figure 4.2 *Effective delegation is not complete without these three pieces of the puzzle.*

If you do not have all three of these parts of the puzzle, you will not get effective delegation. The results will be shoddy ... if done at all. And you will go back to thinking delegation is a waste of time.

The four components in Figure 4.1 labeled 1 through 4 ensure that you have the beginnings of all three parts of this puzzle in place. You start by creating a strong <u>contract of expectations</u>.

COMPONENT 1: CREATE A CONTRACT OF EXPECTATIONS

What?

When you sit down with the person to whom you are delegating a task, you undoubtedly tell her what to do. That is only natural. You tell her the "What" of the task. But all too often, this is where people stop. And frequently, this is not done completely.

In giving the "what?" you need to be sure that you specify not only what the task will be, but also the *complete end product.* And to ensure ownership of the project, be sure to include context and purpose too. My friend George, in delegating the task of picking up the road signs to Dan, told him, "You need to pick up the road signs for the triathlon." In itself, this is not enough information. George also needed to tell Dan to bring the signs to the starting point of the race where they could later be distributed. He also needed (and failed to do so) to tell Dan that he would be responsible for returning the signs to the county roads department.

50

By whom?

The obvious answer to this part of the contract of expectations is the person being delegated to. But as is often the case, the obvious is not always enough. When delegating, make sure that you include all of the <u>peripheral people</u> in the task that are necessary for the task to be completed properly *and* ways they can be contacted.

For instance, Dan needed to know the name of the head of the roads department and his phone number. He also should have been given the names of the owner of the resort where the race was being held so that if there were any problems, Dan would know whom to contact.

It is also crucial to identify the "<u>accountability leader</u>." This is the person you will go to in order to assess the progress or completion of the task. Let us say that Dan knows he will not be available to actually pick up the signs, but his son will. Dan can delegate the carrying out of the task to his son, but in this instance, George will want to make Dan the accountability leader. It is Dan—and not Dan's son—whom George will contact to see if everything is progressing as planned. And it is Dan—and not Dan's son—to whom George will turn if things do not go right.

Often you will need to delegate a task to a team of people. When you do, make sure you clearly establish one person as the accountability leader for the team. An immutable law of life is that when more than one person is accountable, nobody is accountable.

George had also made the mistake of being the person who spoke with the head of the roads department to arrange a time for the signs to be picked up. In doing so, he denied Dan freedom *and* responsibility in the task. In doing so, he absolved Dan (the accountability leader and the "whom" in this project) of his need to be accountable.

51

By when?

When examining where his delegation ran aground, George realized that he had been remiss in a number of areas, but this was the most serious one. Any delegated task needs to have a well-defined outcome and a specific deadline. Although he told Dan when the road signs needed to be picked up, he had not stressed this enough and had not been specific enough in his instructions.

George needed to accentuate that the road signs had to be picked up by a certain time (by noon on Thursday, August 31) or they could not be picked up.

Note how all three of these three factors of creating a contract of expectations work together. By not having the "by whom" clearly delineated as being Dan or the time line clearly specified, George pretty much set this delegation up for failure.

While the term "contract of expectations" sounds formal, in reality, it does not have to be. Depending on the complexity of the task or project involved, the contract can be as simple an oral understanding for simple, short-term projects. You *can* make it more complex if the nature of the project dictates with written and signed time-lines. It is up to you as an effective delegater to decide how strict and structured you need to make the contract.

We suggest, however, that if you do feel that it is necessary to have a written agreement that you express the contract clearly in terms of the three Ws of effective delegation:

And remember, a contract goes two ways. You cannot dictate a contract to someone. It has to be a mutually acceptable agreement. Facetiously we wish we could sometimes. If it were possible we could send a bunch of invoices to various companies. We could then follow it up with invoices telling them if they refused to pay, "Well, we sent you a contract and WE signed it."

That would be ridiculous. The principle is important to remember, however. You cannot send an email, for example, to tell someone what his contract of expectations is. We mention that because we have actually seen that happen. A manager will get upset with a person to whom they have "delegated" because the person did not follow through. Not only was the delegation process incomplete, the other person had not bought into it at the earliest stages because there was no clear contract of expectations.

The 3 Ws of Effective Delegation
What? • By Whom? • By When?

COMPONENT 2: PROVIDE PURPOSE AND CONTEXT

As implied in the last chapter, providing the purpose and context on a task is a necessary part of the initial delegation process. There are two reasons for doing this. First, as I have previously said, providing these two perspectives on a delegated task helps create ownership of the task. By increasing the likelihood of ownership of the task, you will increase the probability of it being completed on time, accurately, and effectively.

The second reason for needing to provide purpose and context is to increase the inspiration and motivation you give to the person to whom you are delegating the task. This happens because he now knows how the task fits in the greater scheme of things; he understands why the task is important. With this greater understanding in hand, he is able to look at different possible ways to perform the task and what outcomes to look for. You have given the person the power to do the work well.

If you are a little fuzzy on what I mean by purpose and context, perhaps the following examples will help.

53

Suppose that you are the head of a newly formed architectural/ engineering firm. The United States Postal Service comes to your firm with a proposal to design new post offices in rural areas to replace the existing window in the general store facility.

After some study of the USPS proposal, you understand the purpose and the context of their plan. The purpose of the plan is to increase the presence of the USPS in rural areas and to improve their service to those communities.

The context is that they are currently serving hundreds of thousands of customers from windows in general stores or similar facilities. The context also establishes that there is enough money to accomplish the project, but the money is limited. This context suggests to you that your firm will not have as much freedom in the design as you would like and the costs of the building must be kept to a minimum.

Your direction to those to whom you delegate the task of designing the rural post offices is that in order to keep the cost down, it will be best to come up with several designs that are essentially cookie cutter designs. You know, and so does your staff, that the resulting post offices will not be very fancy. The work on their design will be mundane and not very sexy.

By giving your designers the purpose and context, they will be better able to come up with reasonably priced designs, but they are also free to design within the purpose and context. They also will be more ready to tackle this rather prosaic project with greater inspiration and motivation because they know purpose and context.

COMPONENT 3: CLARIFY CAUSE AND EFFECT RESULTS

Staying with the USPS project we just discussed, your architects are not thrilled about the work you have delegated to them. When you started this firm, you tried to draw together a bunch of the hottest up-and-coming architects and engineers you could find. You made sure they all shared the same vision as you: quality and imaginative design.

54

Now you are asking them to work on a project that requires little of that special magic that brought you all together. How do you justify this seeming paradox?

By clarifying the cause and effect results.

In this case you explain to your workers that by working on these cookie-cutter designs, you will be able to keep staff employed while everyone waits for the bigger, sexier, and more lucrative contracts.

It can be extremely powerful when you give purpose and context that speaks to the perspective of the team. The above illustration actually occurred in a mid-western architectural firm.

Staff was not too excited about doing these cookie-cutter post offices until they were told the postal service context above and the context that applied to their firm—this job, though mundane, was keeping the firm afloat until a couple of larger, better jobs came off of hold. Also, the firm was able to keep the team in tact with this postal service job not having to have lay offs while waiting for the larger jobs to resume.

By providing your workers with purpose and context and by clarifying the cause and effect results, you have provided them with powerful rationales for working hard and effectively on a project they might otherwise have been sour on.

The same dynamics hold true for less involved projects. In the triathlon example, the purpose of Dan's getting the road signs is to provide safety indicators for cross-traffic automobiles. The context is to decrease the chance of injury to the runners and bicyclists

The cause and effect results of the activity are that a successful triathlon provides the service club with money so they can do community service projects such as providing college scholarships.

55

Again, by providing these purpose/context and cause/effect results, Dan has received more information and consequently more motivation to perform the task effectively and on time.

COMPONENT 4: DETERMINE AND PROVIDE RESOURCES NECESSARY FOR EFFECTIVE COMPLETION

This component of delegation seems like a "no-brainer," but many, many times delegated tasks are not properly carried out because the necessary resources were not provided. Resources can be anything from relevant phone numbers to millions of dollars depending on the nature and scope of the project. Regardless, though, think of the "3 Ts of providing resources" at this stage:

> # The 3 Ts of Resources:
> ## Time • Tools • Talent

At this stage of the delegation process, the important detail is that while discussing the project with teammates, you must create a list of necessary resources. If the list contains more than a few items that are not immediately provided, then you should use a written list. This list is essentially a sub-contract of expectations with the same important components to it as in the main contract of expectations. Specify what? (is needed), by whom (who will provide that resource), by when? (when will the resource be delivered to the person).

Here is a telling example of how lack of resources can impede effective delegation.

There was an environmental firm who performed various field tests – water sampling, soil testing, air monitoring, etc. Staff was frustrated because they didn't have enough equipment to support the amount of projects they had to do and staff trying to work. Management was frustrated because the office wasn't as productive as it needed to be. The irony here was that the delegation system was fairly well enacted except for this component – providing enough resources to do the job.

COMPONENT 5: DETERMINE MONITORING & MEASURING SYSTEM, ESPECIALLY FOR LONGER TIME-LINES

So, now you sat down with the person you are passing on a task to. You have given her a clear contract of expectations. What is next?

We are sure you have heard the old Revolutionary War expression "Trust in God, but keep your powder dry." It is an expression that covers a great many areas in effective organization management, and this holds true for successful delegation as well.

What it means in delegation is simply this: Make sure that you do not leave any details of the process to chance. Even God follows cause and effect principles. Miracles are the exception, not the rule. So if you want to make sure that the tasks you delegate have the appropriate follow-through, you *must* have some sort of system to evaluate the progress and success.

For small, short-term projects the evaluation might be something as simple as a check-in at the expected completion date and time. For more complex projects, you will want to establish and share with the person to whom you are delegating the task a system for monitoring the progress along the way that incorporates an informal or formal measuring system.

For instance, in the case of the triathlon road signs, George has told Dan that Dan will be responsible for calling the head of the county roads department at least a week prior to the event in order to pick up the signs in time. George's monitoring system might be a quick phone call on the Wednesday before the event to see if the initial contact between Dan and the roads department has been made. At that time, George will also determine when Dan plans on picking up the items. Then, as a final check, George can call Dan on Thursday at 10 a.m. to see how things are going. At this time he reminds Dan that they had agreed that Dan would call him when the items are picked up.

A more difficult project would, of course, require a more extensive monitoring/measuring system. Back at the architectural firm design-ing post offices, you might have weekly reviews of progress with indi-viduals or in groups. At that time you would compare the time-line that you had established in you initial meeting with the actual progress being made.

We highly recommend that you make use of a written time-line such as the Delegation Process Form in Figure 4.3 shown on the next page. The form should show the What?/By Whom?/By When? in a way that is easy for all parties to the delegation to understand. It should also have a part for necessary resources, again with the What?/By Whom?/By When? clearly delineated.

The actual tool you use may differ from the one above. What is important is that clear tracking is the important principle to follow. Use whatever form you want but make it clear to all parties involved in the delegation.

ACME CORPORATION
Delegation Process Form

Project Name: _____

Expected completion date: _____

Activity or Product to Be Done (What?)	Person Responsible (By whom?)	Completion Date (By When?)

Resource Tracking Form

Resource to Be Delivered (What?)	Person Responsible (By whom?)	Delivery Date (By When?)

Figure 4.3 A model delegation process tracking form. You do not have to use this particular form. But use some method to keep track of your delegation process ... and do not leave it to chance.

At this point we want to give you a caution. To be an effective delegater it is important to find the balance between micro-management and letting go of so much oversight that you don't provide all that is necessary for completion. We see both but we see more micromanagement than the other. Micromanagement would lead you to plan out every detail in the process that would provide your desired delegated result. When you are delegating you are doing so to a trained professional. (If you are not, then you are entering into a training or coaching interaction that requires a different set of principles, skills and process). Be clear on your outcome, provide the necessary support, and then let go. Micromanagement is negative leveraging, inappropriate, discouraging, as well as wearying and demoralizing to both parties.

COMPONENT 0: RESEARCH THOROUGHLY THE DETAILS OF COMPONENTS 1-5

We come full circle with this section, returning to where we started. Having learned the five components of the initial delegation process, you now have a greater understanding why it is important to prepare yourself prior to meeting with the person to whom you are delegating.

You should be ready to meet with the person fully prepared with a draft contract of expectations (at least a mental one), prepared to give her the purpose and context of the task, able to clarify the cause and effect result, be ready to discuss and facilitate acquisition of necessary resources, and prepared to discuss and negotiate monitoring/measuring systems.

If it sounds complex, it is far less complex if you start out prepared than if you try to muddle your way through the process without prior preparation. The result of this preparation? Clear, clean, effective and hassle-free delegation.

And if it does not work? By preparing yourself at Step 1, you will be able to find the causes and solutions for problems easily. We will see just how easy in our next chapter.

To Recap What You Have Learned In This Chapter:

Proper preparation can make delegation an easy process. The key to making delegation hassle-free is your initial preparation, which includes the following components:

- Research what is needed and prepare for the following activities prior to the initial meeting;
- Create a contract of expectations that stipulates:
  - What? (What needs to be done);
  - By whom? (Including all peripheral people and identify accountability leader);
  - By when? (Be specific);
- Provide concrete examples of the purpose and context of the task;
- Clarify cause and effect results;
- List resources that will be needed for successful completion of the project;
- Discuss, negotiate, and incorporate monitoring/measuring systems.

CHAPTER 5

STEPS 2 – 4: WHAT TO DO WHEN THERE IS POOR FOLLOW-THROUGH

In this chapter you will learn:

- The importance of monitoring and measuring progress
- Four reasons for lack of follow-through
- How to remediate the causes of lack of follow-through
- How to determine the causes of lack of accountability
- When to terminate a person from the team for lack of follow-through

In the last chapter, you learned the five components (well, six really including the "0" component) of initiating the delegation process. When you use this process correctly, you will find that follow-through by the people to whom you are delegating is quite high. Often, all that needs to be done to ensure complete and effective follow-through is including these six components in your delegation process.

But, sad to say, things will go awry regardless of how diligently you follow this first step. When this happens, there is no reason to throw up your hands in despair. Figure 5.1 on the next page shows the part of our Successful Delegation Road Map that deals with this eventuality.

Figure 5.1 looks considerably more complicated than our large-scale map in Figure 3.1. While it is more complex, it is not really more complicated. The three steps are easy to understand and implement.

They are especially easy to implement when you have laid the necessary groundwork for doing so in the first step. If you have done so, you will not have to flounder around looking for the causes of problems. Those causes are generally contained in some misunderstanding, misinterpretation, or lack of some part of Step 1.

As in our previous chapters, we will move through the process step by step even though there will be some repetition from previous chapters along the way.

STEP 2: ASSESS PROGRESS – MONITOR AND MEASURE

In Chapter 3, we labeled this step simply "Assess Progress," whereas here we have expanded the label to include monitoring and measuring. All three aspects of checking to make sure things are going right might seem almost equivalent, but as with much of the entire delegation process, subtle differences exist.

Effective assessment comprises both monitoring and some type of measuring. If you do not incorporate some type of aspect of a monitoring/measuring system, you will be in the exact predicament that my friend George was two days before the triathlon: What needed to be was not done … and it was too late to do anything about it.

If you fail to monitor your delegation, you, too, will probably know too late that things are not going well to be able to effect any remediation of the problem.

You will notice that this step is actually an extension of the last component of Step 1.

As stated in the previous chapter, the complexity of your monitoring/measuring system is largely dictated by the complexity of the project or task. The assignment George gave Dan to collect the road signs for the race was a simple five-step process: Call the head of the county roads department, pick up the items, deliver them to the race site, pick them up at the end of the race, and return them to the county roads department.

SUCCESSFUL DELEGATION SYSTEM

STEP 1

Delegate Accountability

Include Responsibility
and
Authority

STEP 2

ASSESS PROGRESS

0. Research details of 1-5
1. Contract of Expectations
2. Purpose & context
3. Cause & effect results
4. Ascertain resources
5. Monitoring/measuring

63

No or limited follow-through

STEP 4

Renegotiate the contract of expectations

STEP 3

MONITOR

MONITOR

4 REASONS
Lack of:

1. Awareness
2. Training
3. Resources

Provide fulfillment of needs…

4. Accountability

Find perspective and cause

Continued lack of follow-through

Conversation queues to get some clues
Keep issue oriented, not blame-oriented

1. What happened?
2. What caused it?
3. How can *we prevent* re-occurrence?
4. Do you commit to not repeat this?
5. Create tighter future contract & communication

Termination from the team

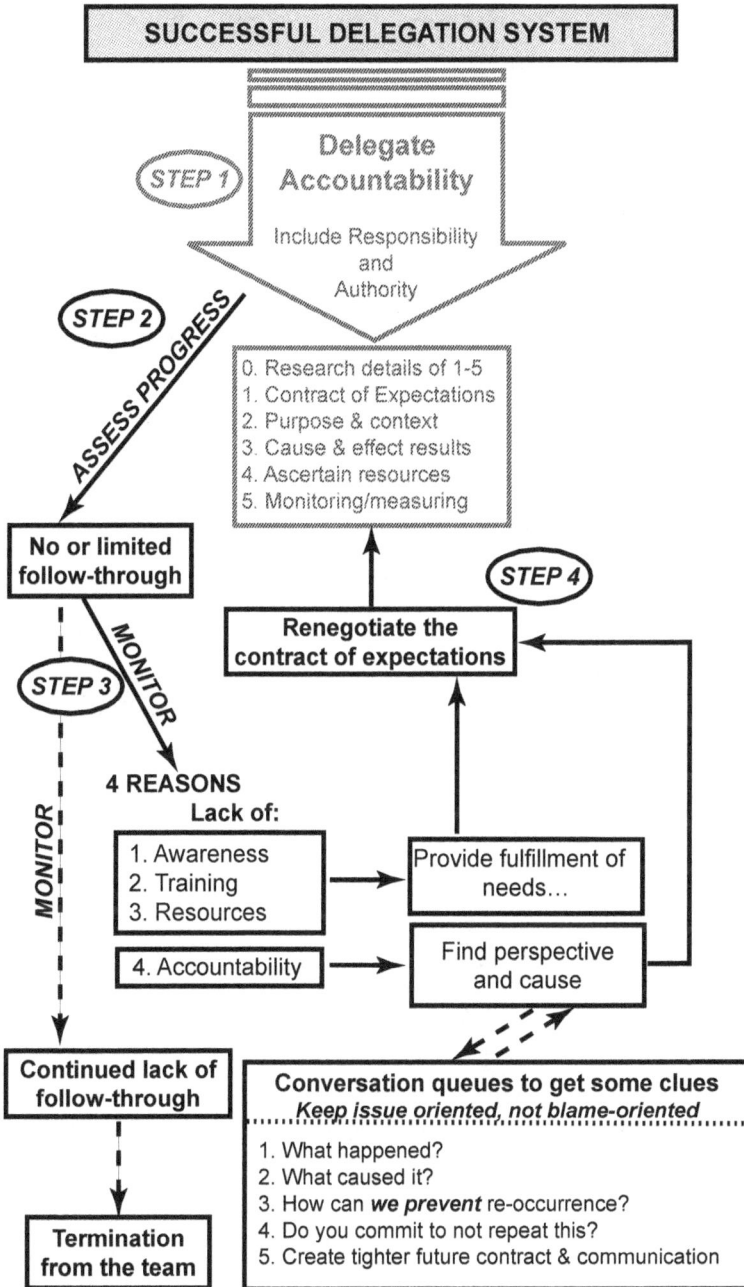

Figure 5.1 Dealing with lack of follow-through can be very frustrating—unless you have a clear road map to guide you where to go and what to do.

George could have monitored progress with a phone call or face-to-face meeting. The measuring involved in this instance could have been a simple "done/not done" check-off of a list. As simple as this task was, the check-off list could even have been a mental one.

A more complex project would need a more complex monitoring/measuring system. For instance, George's job as director of the triathlon could actually be considered a project delegated to him by his service club. In this case, he would be both the overall project manager and the accountability leader.

In a much more complex case such as this, the monitoring system would be proportionately complex. While each monitoring-measuring system will take on its own form, most will have the following structure:

1. Analyze the entire project and break it down into major task areas (task analysis).
2. Determine what large-scale resource areas will be needed for each major task area.
3. Analyze your human resource and make tentative assignments based on people's roles and strengths.
4. Analyze each major task area and develop a list of steps for completion of the task.
5. Delegate each major task to an appropriate person as described in Step 1 of the Effective Delegation System.
6. Negotiate acceptance of the task and establish a list of landmark events with a timeline for completion of each landmark event. (Contract of expectations) Be sure to include discussion and agreement on all parts of Step 1.
7. Use the list of landmark events and the affiliated timeline as the monitoring/measuring tool by which you will assess the partial and final completion of the task.

Essentially what you are doing is task analyzing a project, and then performing a medium-grained analysis of each resulting large task area. Leave the fine-grained analysis to the people to whom you have delegated the task. This gives them the freedom they need to create ownership and to perform effectively.

The medium-grained analysis is valuable for you in that once you have done it; you have your primary monitoring/measuring device with which you will determine along the way whether things are going well.

How long will this process take? Of course that depends on the nature and complexity of the task, but mark our words, it will take far less time than for you to do all of the tasks yourself.

65

STEP 3: DETERMINE REASONS FOR LACK OF FOLLOW-THROUGH

Of course, periodically you will encounter problems where the people to whom you have delegated the task do not follow-through completely or at all on their delegated tasks. There are four reasons for lack of follow-through. These are:

1. Lack of awareness;
2. Lack of training;
3. Lack of resources;
4. Lack of accountability.

The first three of these reasons are relatively easy to remediate; you provide for whatever was lacking in the first attempt. So we will discuss those at this time.

The fourth reason is a bit more complex and requires more work on both of your parts to get the person back on track to successful completion of the task. We will discuss this reason at length later in the chapter. Your monitoring system will give you clues as to which reason or reasons hold for your particular case. Let us look at the first three reasons and see how to remediate them.

1. Lack of Awareness

When your delegated person does not follow-through, ask yourself was he aware of the nature of the task and *all* the elements necessary to complete it properly. In George's case of the triathlon, the biggest reason for Dan's failure to follow-through was lack of awareness. Dan did not have sufficient understanding of the task and its inherent time-lines to perform it well, or in this case, at all.

Remediating this problem is simple. You provide the necessary information. In George's case, he did not have sufficient time to do any remediation, but *he* learned from the experience and was better able to provide all the necessary information (purpose and context, cause and effect results, and an improved contract of expectations) for the next year's event.

In this case, lack of awareness was a problem on the part of both the person being delegated to (Dan) and the delegater (George). This is not an uncommon case, one that you should look out for in your own delegation.

It is not unusual for the *delegater* to lack awareness of the needs of the person to whom he is delegating the task and the degree of understanding of the task that person has. The delegater might also be lacking in sufficient awareness of details of the task to be able to delegate the task effectively.

Again, the case where the delegater lacks awareness of the details is easily remediated. The delegater needs to study the task at hand and understand it in sufficient detail to be able to inform the other person properly.

This does not mean that you need to become an expert on *every* part of a task you will be delegating. That will be the purview of the person to whom you are delegating the task. Your job is to have enough information and expertise in the task to get her started on the down the road to being the task's expert.

In any case, you can create a non-punitive environment that allows for questions. People being delegated to should feel free to ask questions until they have a clear contract of expectations, clear purpose and context—that is complete awareness of the delegated task's components.

2. Lack of Training

If the person to whom you have designated a task does not have sufficient knowledge and expertise, you cannot expect her to do the job well. She may try very hard to do so. In fact, she will probably end up putting in more time and effort than if she did have the necessary training.

67

Let us say that George decides to switch the support jobs around on a yearly basis so that people do not get bored with their current job. (By the way, this is *not* a good strategy for jobs that people do once a year in a case such as this. People develop a sense of pride in doing "their job" as well as improving their expertise on that job. There is little chance of boredom in this case, so George would be ill advised to do this).

This year, George has delegated the task of generating publicity to a Linda an accomplished graphic artist but who has not done this activity for the triathlon before.

One of the sub-tasks that Linda has is to make and distribute flyers at other races to attract contestants to their triathlon. Three weeks after the delegation, George does his agreed upon check-in with Linda to find out if the flyers are ready to be distributed at a footrace the next week. Linda hems and haws but eventually tells George that she has not yet made the flyers, but she will have them in time.

Burned by the fiasco with Dan and the road signs—and a much wiser delegater than before—Dan knows there is a problem. After a few questions, Linda admits that she is uncomfortable using the software she has been given to do the job.

George does not re-delegate this task to another person after talking to Linda. She told him that she enjoyed the task but was frustrated with mastering a piece of software she had never used. Instead of relieving her of her responsibilities, and possibly alienating her, George quickly finds another person who can train Linda on the software.

After being trained on the software, Linda turns out stunning flyers for the triathlon—ones that elicit a better response than any previous flyers.

By providing Linda with the training she needed to complete the task effectively, George has accomplished several things. First, the task was completed to the standard that had been established in the contract of expectations.

Second, Linda feels a strong sense of accomplishment in learning the software. With this accomplishment, she also feels ownership not just of the task but she also feels ownership of the entire triathlon.

Third, Linda feels as if she has received a reward for her work that goes beyond recognition. She has learned skills that she can use in other parts of her life. Learning is one of the ways—and a very powerful way—that people are reinforced for successful follow-through in the delegation process that we will discuss next chapter.

A caveat is necessary here. Frequently when a delegater finds out that the teammate who has been delegated the task lacks the training necessary to complete the delegated task effectively, the impulse is to find someone who has the training. As seen in this example, this is not always the best solution. In fact, if time and resources allow, George's approach of training the person can have a powerful effect on the cohesion of the team.

As mentioned earlier, it is also important to encourage and welcome a person's "I don't know how to do this." This allows for the training necessary to ensure follow through.

3. Lack of Resources

Lack of resources can be the easiest of the problem areas for a delegater to remediate. The obvious solution is simply to provide the necessary resources. However, in some cases resources are unavoidably limited. If that is the case, then that reality needs to be clearly communicated. Using the concepts of teamwork, groups of people can do the "impossible." But if scarcity is not the issue simply providing the resources is the quick and easy fix to this reason for lack of follow through.

When thinking of resources, think in terms of the 3 Ts:

The 3 Ts of Resources:
Time • Tools • Talent

Time is easily understood. Talent is not only the talent the team member possesses but also other talent available to her and you. Tools, however means any item or items that are needed to complete the task successfully and efficiently. These include physical resources, money, as well as information and other intangible resources.

For instance, when Linda finished the flyers, she was supposed to get them distributed to races and sporting goods stores throughout a very large area. She could use other people to help her do the distribution. In the initial delegation, George could tell her whom to contact to help her with the distribution (an information resource) or he could arrange to get people to do the distribution for her (human resources).

If you have done a good job in the initial delegation process of ascertaining what resources will be necessary for the project, then this area should not be a significant problem. However, in large projects, it is seldom possible to anticipate all the resources that will be needed. The *best* way to remediate this problem is to tackle it before it becomes too large. It is far easier for everyone involved if you can provide the missing resources as quickly as possible. For this reason, it is wise for you to make periodic check-ins with the people to whom you are delegating larger, more complex tasks.

STEP 4: RENEGOTIATE THE CONTRACT OF EXPECTATIONS

In summary, when you determine that the reason for lack of follow-through is either lack of awareness, training, or resources, the solution is to provide fulfillment of the needs that you have determined. After you and the team member understand those needs and fulfillment is assured, then a new contract of expectations is negotiated.

However, if you determine the reason for lack of follow-through is a lack of accountability (or acceptance of it), then you have more difficult problems to solve before you try to renegotiate the contract of expectations.

A More Difficult Case: Lack of Accountability

Sometimes, you will find that neither the lack of awareness, lack of training, nor lack of resources is the reason for faulty or no follow-through. Sometimes, the person to whom you have delegated the task does not accept the accountability that is necessary to complete the task.

This situation can be very frustrating for you as a delegater because if you have followed the steps discussed here, you have done everything in your power to make the situation a positive one, one that should end in the desired product or result.

It is very easy to feel angry, betrayed, or disrespected in a situation such as this, but these emotions do not get the problem solved or the task done. You only do that by going through a process involving the reluctant team member that is able to pinpoint the reasons for lack of accountability.

Describing lack of accountability as a *single* reason for poor or nonexistent follow-through is misleading. There are multiple reasons that this can occur and frequently more than one is operating at one time. It is your job to uncover what those reasons could be. Figure 5.2 shows how to do this in a non-threatening, supportive way that also gets results.

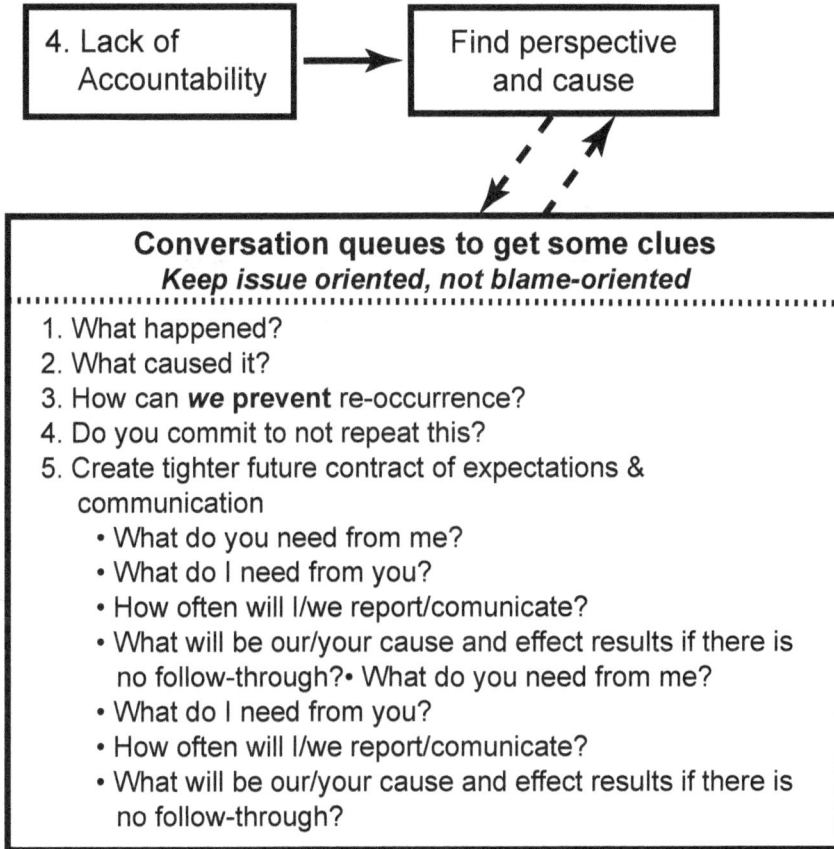

```
┌─────────────────────┐        ┌─────────────────────┐
│ 4. Lack of          │  ──▶   │ Find perspective    │
│    Accountability   │        │ and cause           │
└─────────────────────┘        └─────────────────────┘
```

Conversation queues to get some clues
Keep issue oriented, not blame-oriented
....

1. What happened?
2. What caused it?
3. How can **we prevent** re-occurrence?
4. Do you commit to not repeat this?
5. Create tighter future contract of expectations & communication
   • What do you need from me?
   • What do I need from you?
   • How often will I/we report/comunicate?
   • What will be our/your cause and effect results if there is no follow-through?• What do you need from me?
   • What do I need from you?
   • How often will I/we report/comunicate?
   • What will be our/your cause and effect results if there is no follow-through?

Figure 5.2 In order to remediate lack of follow-through, you must know what causes it.

We call this approach using "conversation queues to get some clues" because the questions that are queued up in a line so that you can get to an understanding and resolution of the problems that caused the lack of follow-through.

The conversation part of the approach means just that. This is not a scolding or a lecture. In order to ascertain the real problems at the base of lack of accountability, you and the other person *must* engage in a true conversation with honest give and take.

It is best for you to enter into this conversation with the issue of lack of follow through as the focal point that both of you need to look at and resolve. Though you want the individual to take responsibility for the lack of accountability, a spirit of blame will only cause the person to be justifying and defensive.

72

We firmly believe the most important aspect of this approach is set down in the second line:

> ## Keep the conversation issue-oriented
> ## *not* blame oriented.

We cannot stress this point strongly enough. As we mentioned above, it is easy to feel angry, betrayed, or disrespected as a leader in a situation like this. You will get nowhere if you bring these feelings into the conversation.

Get a clear perspective that this conversation is *not about you*. It is abut finding a solution to a problem so that your organization, company, or team can benefit, and you will benefit along with it. To accomplish this, though, you *must* put your personal feelings aside.

The way you accomplish this resolution is to ask four main questions.

1. What happened?
2. What caused it?
3. How can *we* prevent re-occurrence?
4. Do you commit to not repeat this?

In the course of answering the first two questions, you will ask many more. But you will note that these questions do not try to place blame nor should any additional ones that you ask. Do not ask "what did you do wrong?" or "how did your actions cause the problem?" Asking like this puts the other person on the defensive, and if this happens, you will spend an inordinate amount of time trying to wriggle out of that morass.

Instead, these questions are not confrontational. The other person *is* being asked to take responsibility with these two questions, but it is done in such a way that the cause is objectified. When this occurs, it is easier for the person to take ownership of his responsibility.

We have an incredible illustration of this in the story of Adam and Eve in the Garden of Eden after they ate the forbidden fruit. Whether you believe Scripture or not, the story is still relevant and dramatic.

God is portrayed as an all-knowing being yet he comes to Adam and Eve after they sinned and asked, "What have you done? Have you eaten of the forbidden fruit?" Though He knew the answers, His questions showed respect for Adam and Eve, allowed them to take responsibility for their actions and entered the conversation in a non-judgmental, non-blaming way.

Once you have established where the problems came from, you and the other person can move on to the third question: How can *we* prevent re-occurrence?

This is a very subtle question. First off, by using "we," you are again not trapping the other person into assuming a defensive posture. Second, it conveys the clear message of support from you. This question is in fact asking the person two questions. The first, most obvious question is asking him how you and he can prevent those events and situations arrived at by the first two questions from recurring.

The second subtle question being asked is how are you and he going to prevent *him* from falling into the traps he fell into previously.

While the first interpretation is objective in its perspective, the second interpretation is more subjective, focusing subtly on the person who accepted the delegation.

Once again, we emphasize that you not blame or force this last interpretation. If you follow this conversation queue, that person will in all likelihood turn the object perspective into a more personal, self-oriented one. He will get to the point of saying "I will ... " when what you asked initially was what can *we* do.

When you reach this point in the conversation, it is time to secure his commitment not to repeat the lack of follow-through. You are *not* asking him not to repeat the things you ascertained as being problems in the first two questions. You are just having him to commit not to have the lack of follow-through.

74

This is important because those first two questions will often times elicit "reasons" that have little to do with the actual delegated process but have more to do with the dynamics of this person's life: sick wife, son's problems in school, demanding work schedule, etc. But in the course of this conversation, you will have come up with core reasons that are pertinent to the whole process as opposed to being centered on the person's life.

Once you have secured commitment from the person not to repeat his lack of follow-through, it is time to build this commitment into a new, tighter contract of expectations and communication.

Communication throughout all aspects of the delegation process is very important and should be part of your general monitoring process. In this case, however, you want to make that communication explicit and understood as being part of the contract.

This new, tighter contract of expectations and communication should explicitly contain the following:

- What do you need from me to succeed in this project?
- What do I need from you to assure your successful completion?

- How often will we report or communicate with each other, and what form will those reports/communications take?
- What will be our/your cause and effect results if there is still no follow-through?

The first three questions here are straightforward and easy to understand and do not need any further explication. However, the last one can be a difficult one for many team leaders. Few of us relish having to put the tight constraints on people that this step requires. We do not like saying "If this happens again, then there will be consequences." It is just not something most of us are comfortable with doing. We would much rather be gracious in all of our dealings with people. But we said it before:

"Graciousness can keep you from greatness."

And graciousness can also keep the people to whom you delegate from greatness as well if, in being gracious, you do not hold them accountable for the results they have contracted to produce.

Consequences are a normal part of life. They keep us on track when we have a goal. Good consequences tell us we are doing the task appropriately. Negative consequences tell us we must change.

If someone to whom you delegate is consistently showing lack of follow-through—even after going through the conversation queues and renegotiating a tighter contract of expectations—that person is holding you and your team back. And he is also holding himself back by his unwillingness or inability to change.

If you do not provide some cause and effect results for his lack of follow-through, you are reinforcing this type of behavior. He will *not* change, to his own detriment.

A person needs to receive the necessary fulfillment for the first three "lacks" only once. However, if there is a second return to the "lack of follow through" box, that usually means a lack of accountability, thus that interaction is engaged.

If a person repeatedly does not follow through because of lack of accountability, it becomes a discipline problem. It is a judgment call on your part as to how many times you let the person cycle through the lack of accountability box to renegotiation before you make the next renegotiation be, " … and if there is lack of follow through next time, you cannot work on the team in the same capacity (or at all)."

What form should this cause and effect result take? Quite simply it should mean termination from the team. This does not necessarily mean termination from employment in a work setting (but it can). But it does mean not being able to work as part of the team in this context at this time.

Going back to the case of the triathlon: If Dan had shown consistent lack of follow-through on getting the road signs, George would be remiss in his own responsibilities if he depended on him to do that or other tasks for the triathlon. If he did so, he would be making other people's jobs more difficult as they had to pick up the slack left by Dan.

Would Dan be kicked out of the service club? Not likely. Termination in this circumstance would entail Dan not being part of the core team that worked on the triathlon. In the renegotiation process, George would tell Dan clearly that if follow-through did not happen again, the triathlon committee would have to look for someone else to do his job.

Dan would be welcome to come to the event and act as one of the "cheer leaders" who encourage the participants as they go through the transition area. The message would be clear. Dan could still be part of the Club and his presence was valued as was he. But he could not be considered part of the core team and would not receive the acknowledgement such participation returns.

If Dan remained in the organization, in the future he may show growth and change and be welcomed back into the triathlon team. Until that time, though, he would have to take a position on the sidelines.

As a delegater of projects or tasks, it is not your job to keep people comfortable and happy. It is your job to see that what needs to be done gets done.

However, a remarkable consequence of insisting on accountability is that people do feel happier in their lives as they attain new levels of competence or receive recognition for the competence they have displayed. As you will see in the next chapter, these are natural consequences of doing a job well and are part of the type of rewards that people receive as a result of following through on their tasks appropriately and effectively.

TO RECAP WHAT YOU HAVE LEARNED IN THIS CHAPTER:

If you follow the component parts of successful delegation as outlined in the last chapter, you will usually have good follow-through by those to whom you delegate. However, this is not a perfect world and you will never get perfect follow-through all the time. When you do not:

- An appropriate monitoring and measuring system will help you track progress so that you can remediate problems as they occur.
- Lack of follow-through occurs because of these four reasons:
  1. Lack of awareness;
  2. Lack of training;
  3. Lack of resources;
  4. Lack of accountability.
- When the lack of follow-through occurs because of lack of awareness, training, or resources, you provide fulfillment of the needs and then renegotiate the contract of expectations.
- When the lack of follow-through occurs because of lack of accountability, use a conversation queue to get some clues as to why. Ask and do the following:

1. What happened?
2. What caused it?
3. How can *we* prevent its re-occurrence?
4. Do you commit to not repeating this?
5. Create a tighter contract of expectations and communication.

- When a person consistently does not show appropriate follow-through on delegated tasks, he must be terminated from the team.

  1. Termination from the team does not necessarily mean termination from work.
  2. Graciousness can keep you from greatness.

CHAPTER 6

STEP 5: REWARD SUCCESSFUL FOLLOW-THROUGH

In this chapter you will learn:

- How to reward follow-through in ways that are congruent with the contribution:

  1. Celebration

  2. Recognition and appreciation

  3. Reward (intrinsic and extrinsic)

  4. Learning

  5. Transfer of knowledge

- Successful follow-through and subsequent reward (by-products):

  1. Build trust

  2. Increase "numbers"

  3. Build team dynamics

  4. Create improvement

So the person to whom you have delegated a task or project has finished it successfully and with good follow-through. It might have been a task that was successfully completed the first time. Or it might have been one that took analysis and remediation. It does not matter; it is now time to celebrate her—and your—success. It is time to reward her in some meaningful way for her efforts.

Things are simplifying in the delegation process since the last chapter as seen in Figure 6.1. As you can see, when there is successful follow-through, *you* follow through with appropriate rewards. The diagram also shows that there are some intrinsic rewards that arise out of the successful delegation process as well as by-products of both success and the accompanying rewards.

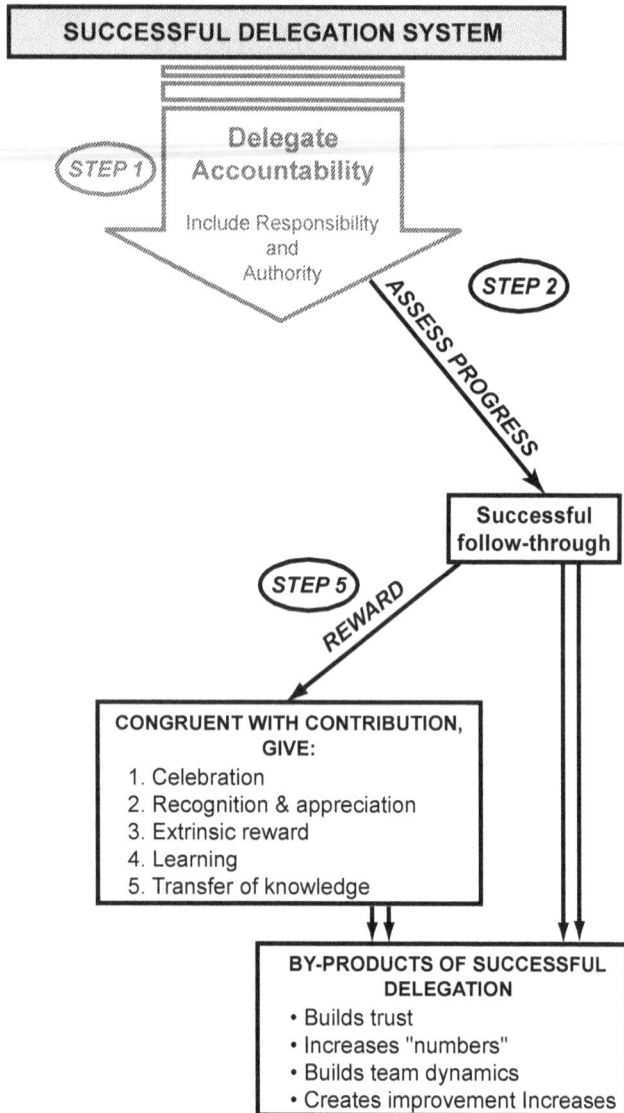

SUCCESSFUL DELEGATION SYSTEM

STEP 1

Delegate
Accountability

Include Responsibility
and
Authority

STEP 2

ASSESS PROGRESS

Successful
follow-through

STEP 5

REWARD

CONGRUENT WITH CONTRIBUTION,
GIVE:
1. Celebration
2. Recognition & appreciation
3. Extrinsic reward
4. Learning
5. Transfer of knowledge

BY-PRODUCTS OF SUCCESSFUL
DELEGATION
• Builds trust
• Increases "numbers"
• Builds team dynamics
• Creates improvement Increases

Figure 6.1 Now comes the fun part ...
rewarding successful follow-through!

It is important to understand how both of these offshoots of delegation work positively for you and your team. Consequently, we will spend a few moments discussing them when it might otherwise seem adequate just to list them. As simple as effective delegation is, one dictum should always apply: Never take anything for granted.

REWARDING SUCCESSFUL FOLLOW-THROUGH

Step 5 in the delegation should come naturally to people. When people complete a task or extend a favor, they should be thanked. Naturally it should be the same in the delegation process.

Unfortunately we've found that people are more courteous to others farther away from them in relationship (grocery store clerk, bank teller) than they are to those closer to them (family members, fellow workers). One of the elements we always find when we do an assessment of an organization is the desire for more appreciation.

Giving the common courtesy of a "thank you" should be done more often, and especially when someone follows through on something you have delegated to him or her.

Consequently—and this cannot be stressed strongly enough—when a team member successfully follows through on a delegated task, you thank and reward him.

The reward *must* be congruent with the complexity and scope of the project that has been completed. If someone has worked on a project for three months that brought your company $500,000 in new business, you would not acknowledge her with a quick pat on the back and a mumbled "thank you" as you passed her in the hallway.

Conversely, if the task was accomplished in thirty minutes with minimal effort, then a 50% raise and television coverage would seem excessive to everyone involved ... including the person who did the work.

Keeping the reward congruent with the job performed is extremely important. If the reward is disproportionately small, the delegater will have trouble garnering support for other efforts. If reward is disproportionately large, other members of the team may feel that the person being rewarded is being shown undue favor. The recipient is also likely to be uncomfortable with the excess praise or reward, wondering why it is being offered and if there is some agenda or later cost to be extracted.

So, bottom line: Keep your reward, praise, and acknowledgment in line with the effort expended and the work accomplished. If you do not it will chip away at trust, both from the person you are rewarding as well as those who are observing.

82

Reward for successful follow-through comes in several forms. You will find yourself using one or more of the following when rewarding your team members. In all likelihood, you will use several or all of them in combination.

1. Celebration

This reward is virtually required of you if you are going to keep your team happy. Celebration could mean a huge party with food, drinks, and dancing … but it seldom does. An appropriate celebration could easily be a handshake and a pat on the back coupled with a few words on your part. Do it sincerely and openly, maybe at a staff meeting so others can participate.

Celebration of this form is in reality one of the strongest reinforcements you can give. We are assuming here that your team member admires and/or respects you. It is highly unlikely that he would not; after all, he has just done work for you. In this case, your praise is a powerful inducement for him to continue working for you.

And if he does not admire or respect you? Well, as we said, it is not likely he would have done the work for you if he did not. But if this is the case, then get someone the person admires and respects (preferably someone with authority in the company or group) to give the kudos as well as your doing it yourself.

One aspect of the celebration principle is the "party factor," the "fun factor." People like to have fun. To the extent you can create it to that extent the celebration can be more rewarding. One company provided sit-down, back and neck massages for a team who had worked exceptionally hard on a project.

Another company had the tradition of buying and bringing fun and funny gag gifts to celebrate the accomplishment of a team member. Still another manager made it a habit of giving a couple of dinner or movie tickets to the person being rewarded so he could have some fun with a person of his choosing.

2. Recognition and appreciation

A few people are satisfied with a word of praise from the delegater and the good feeling that accompanies a job well done. However, most of us like broader recognition for our efforts than that. Again, the degree of recognition depends on the nature of the project. It could be a few words of acknowledgment made at a staff meeting, mention in the company newsletter, or, if the effort is big enough, news coverage.

For the triathlon George wrote individual thank you notes to all the team members, but he also made sure to put their names in the club newsletter that was sent weekly to all members as well as to the club's district governor. George also sent letters of appreciation to the local paper naming those people who had followed through on their commitments.

How you use recognition is limited only by your imagination. In addition to using newsletters and newspapers to honor your team, you can use other media coverage (radio, TV), posters, special days of recognition, a cake with the team members names on it (combining celebration and recognition).

Of course, appreciation must be at the core of any recognition you give. As we said above, make it sincere. If you give appreciation grudgingly at a staff meeting to one of your team members, everyone will sense it.

We saw a wonderful example of showing appreciation in the town where we live. A woman who owns a flower shop provided excellent service and beautiful flowers for a couple's 50th wedding anniversary celebration. The couple bought a rather large amount of space in a local newspaper. In the ad they described the quality of the florist's service and beauty of her arrangements, complete with pictures and a sincere thank you. The florist talked about it for weeks.

3. Reward (extrinsic and intrinsic)

Everything we have been talking about is "reward," but what we are talking about here is something more substantial and more direct.

<u>Extrinsic rewards</u>—coming from outside the recipient—are items such as money, trophies, certificates, cards, special treatment (for instance, special parking), a raise, gift certificates, and the like.

Extrinsic reward can also be the paycheck the team member normally receives. In this case, you would subtly but effectively remind the team member that the task he is being delegated is part of his job description. While you would not be so crass as to express it this way, the message should be clear: "You get a good wage from our company. Successful completion of the tasks delegated to you is one of the reasons you get that pay check." Obviously one possible way to enhance this component is to offer profit sharing.

The high reinforcing value of <u>intrinsic rewards</u>—the various types of "good feelings" that come from inside the person, the feelings of having accomplished something important—cannot be overestimated. These feelings account for the heroic work of Peace Corps volunteers, missionaries, and people who dedicate their lives to service of others.

Research into human behavior has shown that extrinsic rewards have the highest reinforcing value at the beginning of a work relationship (be it for a company, in school, or when involved in a project or task). As the work and the relationship between the parties continues, the intrinsic value of the work and the intrinsic value of the relationship being formed with the other person gets stronger.

But if intrinsic rewards come from within the team member, how is a delegater able to tap into them or elicit them? Paradoxically, this takes place not at the end of the delegation process but at the beginning. Intrinsic rewards that arise because of the nature of the task occur when the team member knows why she is doing the task, that is when she knows the purpose, context and cause and effect results.

85

When you structure a delegation properly using those components, you sow the seeds of the strongest reward the team member will get.

In Dan's case with the triathlon, he basked in the small glory of seeing his name in the newspaper. He appreciated being appreciated and enjoyed the pin that George bought for all the triathlon team. But his ultimate reward came four months later when, as a part of a group of club members, he got to pass out dictionaries to all the third graders in their town—dictionaries purchased partly with money raised at the triathlon. The looks on the children's faces, the words spoken by one little boy as he went back into his classroom saying, "this is my first very own book," these were the rewards that brought him back the next year wanting to do even more.

The extrinsic rewards you choose to bestow are *always* accompanied by rewards that are intrinsic with the process of succeeding at a task. Both extrinsic and intrinsic rewards have immediate and long-term effects that go far beyond those that arise simply out of the completion of the task. Never forget the power of intrinsic rewards and how proper delegation builds them in.

(Right about now you might be feeling a little confused as to the distinctions between celebration, recognition, and reward. A possible clarification would be this: Celebration is the fun/party factor; recognition is what a person receives in the presence of others; and reward is something, internal or external, the delegatee receives for personal satisfaction and/or use. The basic fact is that each of these categories of reward crosses boundaries with the others. They all work together for your benefit as delegater).

4. Learning

Last chapter we told you about Linda, a member of the service club who worked on publicity for the triathlon. We mentioned that one of the reinforcements she got for her work was <u>learning</u> new skills in computer graphic design. Learning is a powerful reward for participating successfully in the delegation process. It can be viewed as an effective combination of both intrinsic and extrinsic reinforcement.

As part of her delegated task, Linda learned new skills that she could use in other aspects of her life, skills that actually increased her value as an employee.

This was an extrinsic "gift" she received because of her participation in the project. By receiving this gift, she also gained an increased feeling of self-confidence and competence, intrinsic gifts that are, once again, powerful reinforcements for her having done her task effectively. This is the norm when learning takes place as part of the delegation process.

Additionally, high performing people and teams are always improving. They do not repeat mistakes and they build on their successes. They look at mistakes as a way of learning … and they have the same attitude about their successes. The only way that can be done is to reflect on what was done, how it was done, what went well, what didn't go well—and to learn from it.

5. *Transfer of knowledge*

Linda learned new skills as a result of her participation in the triathlon. Dan, on the other hand, received a transfer of knowledge. Because of his enthusiastic response to the intrinsic reward he got during the event and while delivering the dictionaries, he wanted to do more for the triathlon. As a consequence, George delegated a larger portion of the event's responsibilities to him, making him co-chair.

Because of this change in position, Dan learned more about the organization of an athletic event, which can be viewed in a narrow context as simple learning. However, the along with the nitty-gritty details of organizing a triathlon, Dan also learned how to delegate responsibility. He learned more about the structure of his local service club and the district service club. He learned the lesson about the value of working toward a goal (raising money at a fundraiser) in order to fulfill another goal (distributing dictionaries).

So, Dan did more than just learn new skills; he was the recipient of the transfer of a large amount of knowledge that gave him a new perspective. A more formal aspect of transferring knowledge comes when individuals or teams overtly tell other individuals or teams in the organization what they have learned. This enables others to not repeat the same mistakes and to build on the successes. When this happens the entire organization is becoming better in a synergistic exponential way.

If you are looking for a defining factor by which you can distinguish between learning and transfer of knowledge it is this: Learning entails acquiring new localized skills. Transfer of knowledge involves a more global acquisition of information, feelings, and perspective in the individual and an overt act of transferring this learning to others.

Just as not everybody who is delegated tasks receives new learning, not everybody receives a transfer of knowledge. But when it happens, it is a powerful reward that frequently "hooks" the team member into being ready to do more, do it better, and do it more efficiently.

MYRIAD BY-PRODUCTS OF SUCCESSFUL DELEGATION

So, let us say you are George. You have put on a successful triathlon. Your team worked hard to ensure its success. You have sent thank you cards, acknowledged people's contribution in newspapers, and given lapel pins to each of them. Several of them are thrilled with the new learning they received and one of your team members is eager to take a much bigger role in the event next year.

Things do not get much better than this, do they?

Oh, yes they do. Figure 6.2 shows how much better things can get.

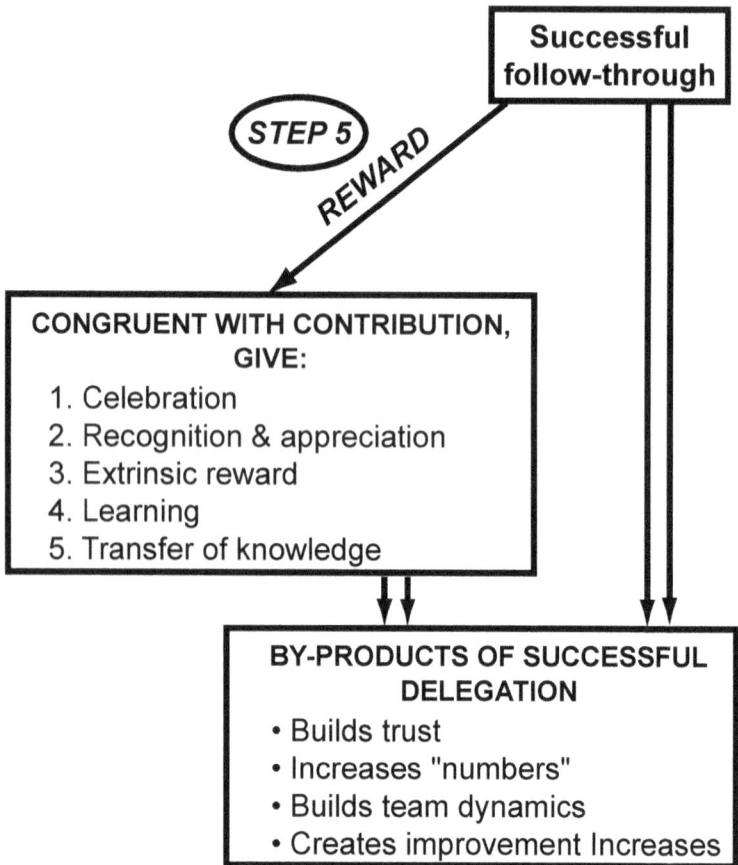

Figure 6.2 Successful delegation and follow-through has many

Successful delegation leads to successful follow-through, which is in turn rewarded appropriately. Successful delegation means a successful project, and from that success offshoots or by-products result. These by-products are not solely a result of the success of the project, nor are they solely a result of the rewarding that goes along with the success. They are a result of the entire process working effectively.

1. Successful Delegation Builds Trust

When you delegate responsibility, in order to be successful you must get people working together. Even if the configuration of people involved is just you and one other person, that person has to invest some trust into the relationship that is developing. His trusting you begins at the very beginning of the process when he accepts the responsibility, authority, and accountability. He trusts that you are giving him the proper information, context, and that you will see that he is provided the resources he needs or information on how to get them.

You are trusting that he will carry out the delegation.

Trust builds trust. When the project is successfully brought to a conclusion, his trust in you is proven justified as is yours in him. Trust builds trust.

2. Successful Delegation Increases "Numbers"

Successful delegation increases the efficiency with which a team works together. In business increased efficiency means greater profitability for the company. And if the company is run on a model similar to this delegation model, increased profitability for the company can mean increased benefits for the employees.

In a group such as George's service club, successful delegation also means greater efficiency. This results in an increase in numbers as well. The numbers here can be financial. A more efficiently run triathlon should draw more participants, require fewer resources, and make more money. But in this case, the financial numbers are less important than "human" numbers. The group will feel a stronger commitment to the club and will attend more meetings, participate in more activities and have more fun. They are also more likely to get other community members to join the club.

3. Successful Delegation Builds Better Team Dynamics

People (at least most people) appreciate success and want to be a part of it. When a task or a project is delegated, the success of the project helps bind people's loyalty to the organization for which they have worked successfully.

In addition, they have had to work together as a team, working toward a common goal. When the project is completed successfully, the work they have done together is rewarded both extrinsically and intrinsically. The result: Better team dynamics. People will work better and more effectively together.

4. Successful Delegation Creates Improvement

We have been involved in facilitating personal and organizational growth for over twenty years. In that time, one thing has become evident. It is far easier to create and foster improvement in people or an organization when they experience success. There are many reasons for this, but one of the key ones is that success is habit forming.

And this is a habit that is decidedly good for you. You can see this operating in top athletes such as Jerry Rice of the San Francisco 49ers and Oakland Raiders.

When Jerry was at the very peak of his career, sportscasters would marvel at how hard he practiced, always getting to the field before his teammates to practice passing and blocking routes he had run literally thousands of time before. Why was he so driven? Partly his personality, but partly because his previous successes created a need in him to improve.

This dynamic holds for all truly successful businesses and people. Effective delegation helps create an atmosphere where people want to go beyond their previous successes, where they strive for improvement. This quest for improvement may start small, but success, even small-step success, is a power inducement to improve.

We have reached the end of the road map. You now know the steps and components necessary to delegate responsibility, authority, and accountability so that people will work effectively for the benefit of everyone involved. Our next chapter, a very short one, describes the three types of delegation based on real and perceived power roles.

TO RECAP WHAT YOU HAVE LEARNED IN THIS CHAPTER:

If you follow our simple road map for successful delegation, your team will experience far more successes than they thought possible. When they are successful, it is important to provide rewards that are in line with the efforts and contributions that have been made. Successful delegation produces by-products that strengthen the organization. Here is a summary:

- Reward follow-through in ways that are congruent with the contribution:
  - Celebration can be as simple as a handshake and a "job well done." It can also be more extensive.
  - It is crucial to give recognition and appreciation. Virtually everybody appreciates when they are appreciated.
  - Rewards can be extrinsic (coming from outside the person) or intrinsic (coming from within the person). Intrinsic reward is subtler but is often stronger and can be life-changing. Intrinsic reward flows from the very beginning of the successful delegation process.

- When people learn new skills as part of the delegation process, the learning can be both an extrinsic and intrinsic reward. Learning new skills helps increase an individual's sense of self worth and competence.

- Transfer of knowledge is a global experience that empowers people to take on new and changing roles in their lives.

• Successful delegation and its subsequent reward:

- Builds trust among those who have worked together as delegater and team members;

- Increases "numbers" including financial, group, and personal;

- Builds team dynamics by facilitating success while working as a team;

- Creates improvement because success breeds success and success is habit forming.

CHAPTER 7
THREE WAYS TO DELEGATE

In this chapter you will learn:

- Three ways to delegate:
  - Down
  - Sideways
  - Up
- The delegation process remains the same for all three ways to delegate.

93

Usually when people think about delegating tasks, they imagine doing so as part of a work setting where someone in a higher level of authority delegates to someone in a lower level of authority. We refer to this type of delegating as "delegating down" (that is, down in the context of an organizational chart). It is in some respects the easiest delegation because you, the delegater, have leverage with the person to whom you are delegating the task.

Delegating down is only one of three ways that responsibility can be delegated. You can delegate responsibility sideways to people of the same level of authority as you. The story we have been following of George and the triathlon is an example of sideways delegation.

You can also delegate up to people who have a greater authority than you do. Each of these ways of delegating follows the same process as you have just learned. The way you would approach the individual to whom you are delegating will differ, however.

DELEGATING DOWNWARD

As we mentioned above, you have greater leverage with a person when you are delegating down. You follow the same structure as we have discussed previously through all phases of the process. Your approach with the person must be respectful and collegial, but you should maintain a fair degree of professionalism.

Be careful not to blur the lines of authority in establishing the delegation relationship.

If the person to whom you are delegating demonstrates lack of accountability, you have the power in this delegation scenario to provide sanctions that can enforce acceptance of the accountability.

Use this power sparingly but do not be afraid to use it. Do not forget that "graciousness can keep you from greatness."

DELEGATING SIDEWAYS

Most of the delegation you will do in your nonprofessional life (and much of it in your professional life) will be sideways. The people we are asking to help us by taking on a task are our equals in terms of our power relationships with them.

Once again, you follow the same components for successful delegation. But in this case, your attitude of being respectful, courteous and tactful every step of the way is your most powerful tool.

When delegating sideways, it is best to ask questions that lead to the answer you are seeking rather than command or confront. For instance, in getting Dan to accept the task of collecting the road signs, George would start out by explaining the task to Dan. He should then ask Dan if he has enough help and, if not, what does he need to help him make this a successful event.

DELEGATING UPWARD

You are likely to be in this situation in a work or professional context. Let us say that a supervisor who is two levels up from you has delegated a project to you. He has not left strict instructions that *you* are to complete the project just that it must get accomplished by May 31.

In looking at the project, you realize that you lack some of the necessary skills and there is not enough time for you to learn them, do your normal job, and work on this task. So you go to your immediate supervisor and tell him, "I cannot do this because [insert whatever reason is real]. Can I give it to you or have you give it to someone who does have the skills necessary?"

As with sideways delegation, you must—absolutely must—be tactful, courteous, and respectful when delegating up. After all, your job depends on it. Again use questions to move the process along. The "power of the question" is a power few people use. Tactful, respectful, courteous questions—asked with genuine sincerity—cause the other person to have to answer them. This enables you to walk them through the delegation process without their knowing about it, be it something you are asking them to do for you or something they are asking you to do. The components you ask about, such as the specifics of the what, by whom, by when; will be received well, however, because they are important to the person delegating to you.

An example of delegating up just happened while writing this. One of our clients called to ask questions regarding the possibility of our doing some more work for him. He would be above us in the power position since he is the one hiring. We needed some information from him in order to proceed, thus we "delegated" the task to him. In so doing we tactfully asked the appropriate questions thus engaging the delegation system, "Steve, when will you be able to provide us with that information? How will you give us the information, do you want to call or email it?

Not all upward delegations are in a professional or work context. You might be delegating a task to the minister of your church, or a highly respected member of the community, or your daughter's soccer coach. These examples seem as if they could conceivably be examples of sideways delegation, but they are not.

In cases such as these, there may be no real difference in the power roles each of you plays in your professional lives, but there is a difference based on the relative position of respect or power within the community. Note here that in the case of the soccer coach, the coach's power position relative to you is based not on his actual relationship to you. It is based on his relationship with your daughter. That does not change your relative power position in respect to him. He is above you as long as your daughter remains on his team and as long as you wish to maintain a good relationship with him. (The context is, of course, limited to activities relating to the soccer team). You could, of course, break that relationship with a few words, but you would probably jeopardize your daughter's position on the team if you did so.

We bring this example up as a reminder to your to do you homework before going into the delegation process. One of the factors you must consider carefully is exactly what your relationship with the other person is. Once you have determined that, then you are well informed on how best to approach the person.

Now that you have seen how well delegation can work when this process is followed, it is time to revisit ineffective delegation to see what threats there are to effective, successful delegation, which we will do in our next chapter.

To Recap What You Have Learned In This Chapter:

- There are three ways to delegate. The delegation process remains the same for all three ways to delegate but your approach will vary:

96

- Down – to people whose relative power or responsibility is less than yours; this occurs frequently in your professional or work setting. In this case, you can use your relative position as some leverage if necessary.

- Sideways – to people on an equal or quasi-equal power level as you. Delegating to these people must be done with tact and courtesy.

- Up – to people with actual power differences (your supervisors and bosses) or relative differences by virtue of their position in the community. Delegating to these people takes tact, courtesy, and grace. Both 2 and 3 are done with the power of the question.

97

98

CHAPTER 8
THREATS TO SUCCESSFUL DELEGATION: AVOIDING THE PITFALLS AND TRAPS.

In this chapter you will learn:

- Even though you follow the delegation process you have learned here, successful delegation can be threatened by the following process threats:

    1. Lack of talent,

    2. Weak contract of expectations,

    3. Insufficient resources,

    4. Over-delegation,

    5. Unclear delegation,

    6. Responsibility without authority,

    7. Multiple accountability trails.

- Psychological threats to successful delegation include fear of:

    1. Loss of control and recognition,

    2. Loss of importance and identity,

    3. Not getting it done right.

You have been given a set of tools in the previous chapters that allow you to delegate tasks and projects so that they will be completed successfully and efficiently. Does this mean that *all* your delegation attempts will be successful and that the process will run smoothly from start to finish? Hardly.

You will encounter problems along the way. After all, you are dealing with humans and not computerized automatons, which, let us remind you, is a good thing although it does not always seem that way. You *will* run into problems along the way that can become threats to successful delegation.

These threats fall into two major categories: <u>process threats</u> and <u>psychological threats</u>. Process threats are those that arise because of some problem or deficiency within the delegation process itself. Psychological threats are those that arise from within you or the team member to whom you are delegating.

PROCESS THREATS TO SUCCESSFUL DELEGATION

There are seven major sources of process problems that you need to watch for when you are delegating. These are:

1. Lack of talent,
2. Weak contract of expectations,
3. Insufficient resources,
    - Time
    - Tools
    - Talent
4. Over-delegation,
5. Unclear delegation,
6. Responsibility without authority,
7. Multiple accountability trails.

1. Lack of Talent

Lack of talent means one of two situations exists. Either the person you have chosen for the task lacks the learning necessary to accomplish it well. In this case, if time permits, you provide the training needed.

The second more serious situation occurs when the person you have chosen lacks the innate talent to do the job. For instance, you may have chosen a man to do the bookkeeping for a project who is inept when it comes to working with numbers. Lack of talent does not mean this person is inept in everything. Perhaps this man is a talented and passionate writer, but the only way he can balance his checkbook is if his 12-year old son does it for him

In cases such as this, you simply have to bite the bullet, admit you chose the wrong person for the job, and re-delegate. Of course this will often take sensitivity on your part to do it. We are sure the hapless bookkeeper will be happy to give up his position ("What *were* you thinking?" he is likely to say).

But let us say you have delegated the task of designing a logo to someone who has no apparent talent for graphic design ... realized of course *after* you made the choice. The woman who took the job fancies herself a top-notch amateur graphic artist, so of course she was thrilled when you handed it off to her. Once you see her draft designs, you realize she lacks the talent, and she is not about to learn the skills necessary or have some divine intervention to give her the talent she will need to do the job satisfactorily.

What do you do? Well, as we said, you must employ tact in this case. One suggestion we have is that if this person has obvious talent in another area, you find a job in that area to delegate to her. Perhaps she is the group's best musician. You come to her and apologize profusely. You acknowledge and celebrate the work she has done thus far on the logo design, but right now, she is really needed to help organize the staff talent show that she will star in.

Once you make this clever sidestep, you go through the entire delegation process around both projects and hope that this works.

Sometimes you will not be able to make this type of graceful maneuver and are faced with having to deal with the problem head on. How you do it depends on what the context of the delegated task is.

You have greater latitude in how you deal with the person if you are delegating within a work setting. It may be necessary to tell the person directly that he lacks the talent to work in this particular domain. You would want to back it up with facts, but at the same time you want to be kind, tactful, and courteous. It is helpful, though not always possible, to be ready to offer the person another assignment or position.

You are doing the other person a favor. He may already be sensing his inadequacy but feels he is trapped where he is. A situation such as this can be one where you are able to get the delegated task back on target while at the same time providing the possibility of positive change to the person you have removed from the project.

And sometimes you have no choice. You are forced to terminate the person from the team. Again, this should always be done tactfully and with suggested resources for the person so that she does not feel overwhelmed by the circumstances.

The way to avoid this pitfall is to do an informal inventory of your team to find out their areas of true (as opposed to self-perceived) talent. Draw on that real talent pool when delegating.

2. Weak Contract of Expectations

If your initial contract of expectations is not structured enough, you can easily run into problems with your delegation. Check to see if you have clearly stated these components:

- What: Have you clearly stated what the end product is to be? Have you ascertained that the team member understands?
- By whom: Have you identified all the people who will share in this project or task including peripheral people? Have you clearly identified the accountability leader (AKA the "point person")?

- By when: Have you clearly stated the absolute deadline for the project's completion? Have you established check-in deadlines as well?

If you sense that a weak contract of expectations is bedeviling your delegation, immediately (or sooner) go back and renegotiate the contract. Failure to do so means that you are almost certain to end up with sub par products or outcomes … if you get any at all.

The way to avoid falling into this trap is to always establish strong, structured contracts of expectations. If a team member is trying to negotiate his way out of a strong contract, he might not be the right person for the job. Alternatively, he may feel that he lacks some of the resources he needs. It is up to you to determine why he wants a weaker contract and to not compromise on the strength of the one you finally settle on.

103

3. Insufficient Resources

Ask yourself, "Have I provided my team member with the time, tools, and talent he needs to complete the delegated task well? Has he accepted the resources offered to him?

Do not forget that in this context, tools mean all the physical resources he will need including, but not limited to, money, supplies, space, tools, etc. In this context, talent does not mean his own innate ability to get the job done. Rather it refers to whether he has sufficient human resources available to do so. If you have not supplied the necessary resource, do so. If you have and the delegation is still not going as it should, you are probably back to a case of lack of accountability. Review what you learned in Chapter 5 on how best to deal with that situation.

4. Over-Delegation

This pitfall has two faces. The first arises when you have delegated too much to one person. When you swamp someone with responsibility above her level of ability to work effectively, you will inevitably get shoddy or incomplete follow-through. The answer is obvious. In the first place do not overwhelm a person with too much. And if you accidentally do, then tactfully get that person out from under the burden.

Make it clear to her that *you* made the mistake of giving her too much work. Be careful to avoid expressions such as "too much for you to handle" that can make your team member feel inadequate. Instead, take the responsibility on yourself. Say, "I made a mistake. I gave you an excessive amount of work, and I want to make it right."

104

The other face this trap can take is when the delegater delegates too much to various team members. In other words, he gives too much of the responsibility away and spreads the work around too thinly with too many micro tasks distributed to too many people, tasks that could be easily lumped into a "project" for one person.

The danger in this is that the delegater risks losing contact and subsequent control of the overall project for which he is ultimately responsible. You can see this type of thing happen in poorly managed corporations where projects and responsibility have been spread so thinly that no one knows who is really responsible for what. There is simply too much to keep track of.

There is no absolute number where this can happen. The optimum number of delegated tasks will depend on the person doing the delegating and the nature of the overall project and micro-tasks. Some people are able to manage many more delegated projects than others. Some projects are easy to break into many micro-tasks and still be manageable, and some are not.

The importance is for you to get a feeling for how much delegation is too much for you. If you find yourself running around trying to evaluate accountability and are unable to get a clear picture of what is really going on, then you have probably over-delegated.

5. Unclear Delegation

This delegation trap pretty much speaks for itself. If you do not give your team members clear directions as discussed in Step 1 (Chapter 4), you cannot expect them to fill in the blanks. If this is the case, then your lack of clarity indicates that you do not understand the task. It shows that you have not taken Step #0 and done your homework. How do you avoid this trap? It is quite simple:

Do your homework *before* you delegate.

6. Responsibility without Authority

We have all been put in this position at one time in our life or another where we have been charged with a responsibility but not given the authority to see that it gets done. And we bet you hated it as much as we did.

Another friend of ours provides a good simple example of how frustrating this can be. Sam volunteers every week at the local junior high school. He is well liked and respected by the kids. One day, the teacher asked him to watch the class for fifteen minutes while she met with a parent.

Sam did not have any problems with most of the class. They played the game the teacher suggested. However, one student who was new to the class became disruptive. When Sam tried to quiet him down, the boy said something to the effect of "I don't have to do what you say. You're not my teacher." And he was right, at least at that time. Most of the other kids resented this boy's attitude and told him so, but a few of the students joined in the disruptive activities.

Sam was stuck in a position with responsibility without authority. It was a long fifteen minutes. Sam rectified the situation. When the teacher returned, he asked her to tell the students that when he was the lone adult in the class like that, he had all the authority of a teacher. She gladly told them and from that time, he has not had a problem.

The lesson for you in this is to make sure that you give the team member to whom you are delegating enough authority and you ensure that those whom this person has authority over know it too. Perhaps this means putting a club member's name on a charge account at the grocery store. Or maybe it means giving an employee full access to the company's printing facility. It does not mean giving the person carte blanche to do as he pleases or to become a tyrant with his coworkers. But it does mean delegating enough authority to get the job done effectively and on time. In reality, when you delegate something to someone, they stand in your stead therefore you need to ensure that the same dynamics should occur as if you were doing the task.

7. Multiple Accountability Trails

This pitfall is the flipside of over-delegation. All too frequently, people in business are so concerned about CYB (covering your behind), that they designate multiple accountability trails so that virtually everybody above them is involved in overseeing the project.

In delegating a task, a delegater in this position will tell Susan to check with Jane and him every week, and then stop in every two weeks and talk with the district supervisor. And, just to be on the safe side, leave a copy of her progress with the CEO's executive secretary.

Whereas in over-delegation there might be no single authority to turn to, in this case there can be so many that the poor team member does not know whom to listen to or talk to if there is a problem. She will be getting suggestions and direction from numerous people, some of which may be contradictory. Who is her final authority? Whose direction is she responsible for incorporating in the project? Who does she get the final okay from?

If Susan does not have clear answers for these questions, she is being asked to follow a circuitous accountability trail and, like Hansel and Gretel, she will get lost. It is our belief that every accountability trail has only one path. There may be trails of information to someone else, there may be communication trails to others, there may be inquiry trails to still others—but there is only one accountability trail.

PSYCHOLOGICAL THREATS TO SUCCESSFUL DELEGATION

Psychological threats to delegation are not as easy to spot or avoid as are process threats. They reside deep within the people involved in the delegation process and often do not come to the surface readily. Be aware, too, that while you can expect these threats to exist within the people to whom you are delegating, they can also be in you.

The most common psychological threats to delegation are around the issue of fear. They are:

1. Fear of loss of control and recognition,
2. Fear of loss of importance and identity,
3. Fear of not getting it done right, resulting in:
   • inefficiency
   • loss of client or customer

You can see how these fears can be your fears as well as those of the person you are delegating to. They are all straight forward and do not need any explanation. The problem comes not in understanding them but in knowing how to deal with them when they pop up.

One word of explanation needs to be given, however. The fear of loss of control and recognition is usually manifested in a person's words surrounding whether he really has authority or not, or how others will know about this authority. Another way it is manifested is in the person expressing fears of their regular work not getting done because of this delegated task.

Fear of loss of importance and identity can be manifested in a person saying this job or task really should be someone else's, that it really doesn't use their talents fully, or that it really isn't a part of their job description.

Fear of not getting it done right is usually expressed as just that. Even with clearly stated expectations and overt support of the appropriate resources associated with your words of belief in the individual – there is still fear expressed.

If you suspect that these fears might prevent adequate follow-through by your team member, the best way to deal with them is directly and at the time of the initial delegation ... at Step 1 or the minute you see them surface.

Do not call them fears to the team member because she will deny them. Address them directly, though, and tell her how she will get recognition and maintain control, how her importance and identity within the organization will increase, how the system you have set up ensures support toward a successful completion of the delegated task or project.

Sounds easy ... and it is. It *is* easy when you are dealing with another person. However, these fears are hard to allay when they are your own. Let us take a look at them as they apply to you, the delegater.

Loss of Control and Recognition

As a hard working, highly responsible person you do not want to lose control of projects that are under your control. You feel your reputation depends on the accurate discharge of your responsibilities. However, if you establish a strong contract of expectations when delegating, you still retain a great deal of control of a project, albeit at a distance. And if your monitoring/measuring system is good, you will not lose that control.

As far as recognition is concerned, you *will* get credit. But it will be for higher-level skills than if you tackled the project on your own. If you are able to delegate successfully, your reputation for being able to manage projects effectively will expand to encompass a reputation for being able to manage people effectively, too.

If you lose out to this fear you will find yourself micromanaging, frustrated and fearful, then re-doing the delegated task anyway – all wasted effort.

Loss of Importance and Identity

Likewise, as your reputation as a manager of tasks, projects, *and* people increases, your importance will also increase. You will not lose your identity. It will evolve into an identity that carries with it greater options for person and professional growth.

If you find yourself concerned about lack of importance or identity, that usually indicates a self-esteem issue. It may be well for you to do some work with a qualified professional to develop a stronger, healthier self-esteem.

Fear That the Project Will Not Be Done Right

Once again, your contract of expectations and the monitoring systems you establish protect you from the problems this fear encompasses. This is more of a straw man than anything else. All that it takes to disprove the basis for these fears is to go through the delegation process several times. You will find that the amount of work you put in versus the amount of time you save, coupled with an increased reputation for being a people manager, will sweep this fear away.

In each of these cases it takes a true "letting go" to be a successful delegater, which is a wonderful way of showing respect and trust in other human beings on your team.

TO RECAP WHAT YOU HAVE LEARNED IN THIS CHAPTER:

- Successful delegation can be threatened by the following process threats:
    1. Lack of talent. When this occurs you must either

train for the talent that is lacking or reassign the task. Prevent it by doing an informal inventory of the talents your team members possess and delegate accordingly.

2. Weak contract of expectations. When this occurs, renegotiate the contract. Prevent this by establishing a strong contract of expectations at the beginning of the delegation process.

3. Insufficient resources: Provide or facilitate getting any of the following that will be needed for successful completion.
   - Time
   - Tools
   - Talent

4. Over-delegation. This can make it difficult for team members to know exactly who is in charge of the project. Avoid it by carefully studying your team and the projects you are delegating. Make sure you have not given too much work to one person nor delegated too widely and extensively.

5. Unclear delegation. Begin at Step 1 with a clear description of your contract of expectations and clarify as needed along the way.

6. Responsibility without authority. Make sure you give the necessary authority to the team member to get done what needs to get done. You do *not* have to give carte blanche authority in doing this.

7. Multiple accountability trails. These can prevent the team member from knowing to whom she needs to listen for direction and feedback. Prevent this by establishing simple, linear accountability trails.

- Psychological threats to successful delegation include fears for both the team member and the delegater. The fears of the team member can be easily allayed in the initial delegation process (Step 1) and along the way. The fears of the delegater are best allayed through practice. He will find that he does not experience:

1. Loss of control and recognition. In fact, he will be perceived as being an effective manager of projects *and* people.

2. Loss of importance and identity. Likewise, her identity will evolve into one of a person having higher-lever skills.

3. Not getting it done right. Within a few times using this process, delegaters find that things get done more efficiently, faster, and with better satisfaction all around.

CHAPTER 9
SUCCESSFUL DELEGATION SUMMARIZED

Successful delegation is no accident. It comes about when the delegater—you—takes the time to assure that it will succeed. As you have seen, the process is not difficult, but you will need to give thought to each step in the process to make sure you get top-notch results.

IN SUMMARY

Successful delegation can be broken down into five steps summarized below and mapped out once again n Figure 9.1 on the next page.

STEP 1: DELEGATE ACCOUNTABILITY

When you delegate, be sure to include responsibility and authority. Create a strong contract of expectations covering <u>what</u>, <u>by whom</u>, <u>by when</u>. When first discussing the delegation with your team member, include purpose and context, clarify cause and effect results, determine necessary resources, and establish a monitoring/measuring system so you can track follow-through.

STEP 2: ASSESS PROGRESS

Your monitoring/measuring system will tell you if the delegation is working. If there are problems with follow-through, you then move to the next step.

114

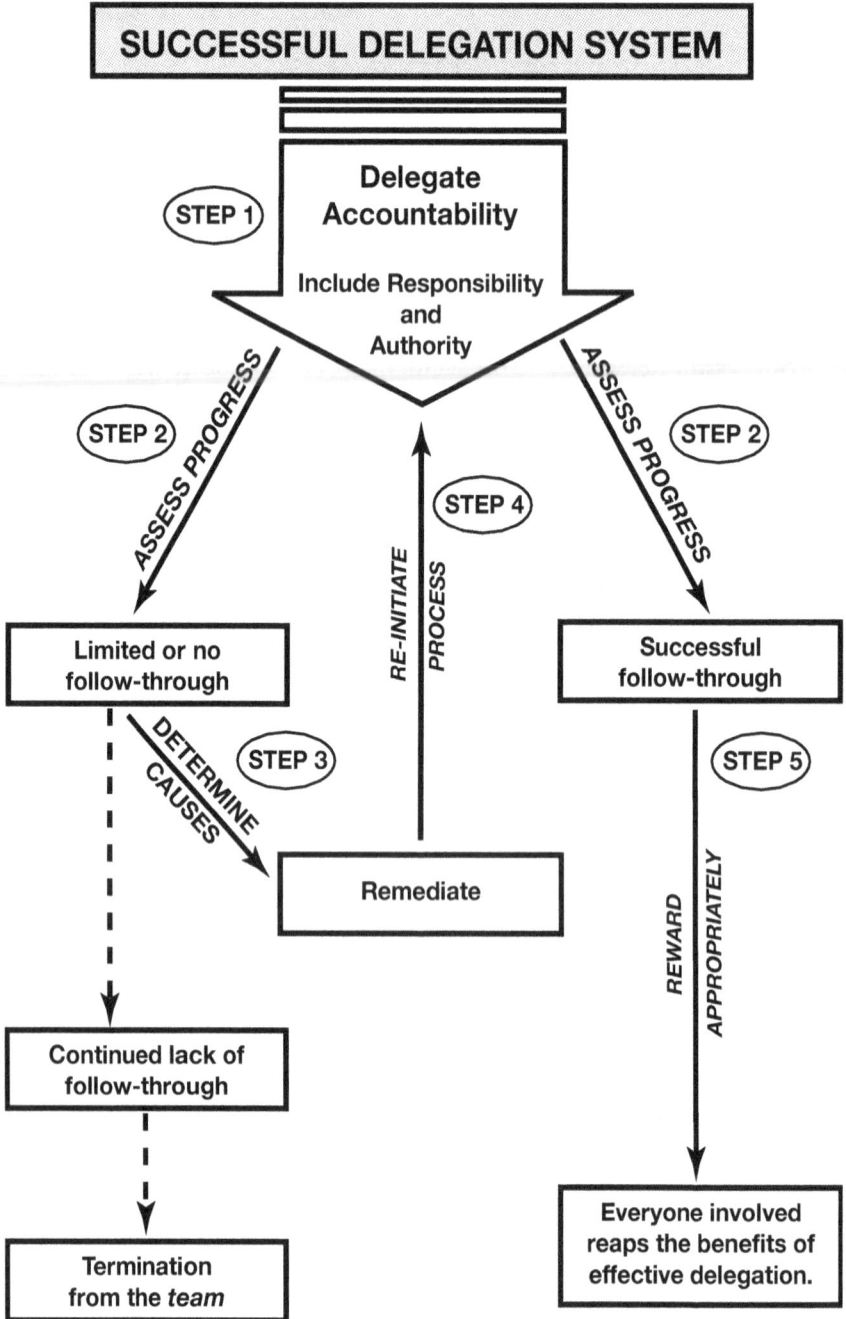

Figure 9.1 The delegation process summarized

STEP 3: DETERMINE THE REASONS FOR LACK OF FOLLOW-THROUGH

There are four reasons for lack of follow-through:

1. Lack of awareness: Rectify this by explaining the purpose of the task and what needs to be accomplished for it to be a successful project.
2. Lack of training: Provide the necessary training or reassign the project.
3. Lack of resources (time, tools, and talent): Supply them as needed.
4. Lack of accountability: Use issue-oriented language and approach rather than a blame-oriented one. Determine:
   - what happened,
   - what caused it,
   - how can we prevent its re-occurrence.

When you have finished these conversation queues to get the clues, create a tighter contract of expectations.

STEP 4: RE-INITIATE THE PROCESS

Start by renegotiating your contract of expectations, then return to Step 1.

STEP 5: REWARD

When you have good follow-through, you want to reward your team and the members of the team who did the work. The rewards must be congruent with the team member's amount of work and contribution.

Rewards can take the form of one or more of the following:

- Celebration: This may be as simple as a handshake and a spoken word of appreciation. It can also take much more elaborate forms. You *must* have some form of celebration, and stir in some fun

- Recognition and appreciation: This is a must!
- Reward: commensurate with the amount of work put in. (Reward can be the person's paycheck). Rewards can be both extrinsic and intrinsic. Intrinsic rewards are usually the strongest.
- Learning new skills
- Transfer of knowledge

BY-PRODUCTS OF SUCCESSFUL DELEGATION

The following occur as by-products of successful delegation:

- Builds trust between the delegater and the person to whom the task was delegated
- Increases "numbers" (productivity, profit, fun, morale, etc.)
- Builds team dynamics
- Creates improvement

As you recall, there are many reasons for you to want to delegate. When you are able to delegate effectively and successfully, you are able to do more things in your life that you want to do rather than being stuck doing things you feel you have to do.

If you choose not to delegate—if you choose instead to let demands on your time determine the quality of your life—you will be stuck doing what you have always done: working harder, getting less enjoyment out of life, increasing your stress, damaging you relationships with others, and impacting your health and well-being.

So, make the intelligent choice for *your* life. Delegate using the system you have learned here and free yourself from the tyranny of unmet schedules, unreasonable demands, and unmet hopes and aspirations.

CHAPTER 10
GLOSSARY

The following terms occurred throughout this book and were underlined at their first occurrence. The number in brackets refers to the chapter where the term first appeared.

Accountability: responsibility to someone else or to others, responsibility of the successful completion of a task. [3]

Accountability leader: also known as the "point person;" the person specifically charged with the completion of a task. This person is the one to whom the delegater and others will go in order to determine the status of the project, degree of follow-through, and resources needed. This is the person who will be rewarded for successful completion or follow-through and who will be held accountable if follow-through is incomplete or nonexistent. [4]

Buy-in: the process of accepting an organization's purpose as ones own, increasing one's commitment and stake in a task, group or organization. [3]

Context: the specific details about a task or project that give additional information to the person doing the task that allow him to make judgments on how best to carry out the assignment. [4]

Contract of expectations: contract with someone charged with completing a task that contains specific information on What (specific description of the task or project to be completed), By Whom (the person receiving the delegation and all peripheral people necessary to complete the task), and By When (specific timeline for completion of tasks and sub-tasks, depending on complexity of the project) [4]

Extrinsic: coming or operating outside something or someone [6]

Extrinsic reward: reward for performance or follow-through that comes from outside the person doing the task; rewards such as money, special privileges, prizes, etc. [6]

Family dynamics: the often negative or inappropriate ways that family members interact with each other. This includes lack of accountability, lack of open communication, and lack of shared ownership. Family dynamics are not appropriate in organizational structures and should be discarded. [3]

Family values: positive values that occur in the family that include love, trust, support, and caring. Family values should be encouraged, nurtured, and honored organizational structures. [3]

Freedom: in the context of successful delegation, the ability or authority to act of ones own volition and purpose within established parameters. [3]

PCIM: Purpose, Context, Inspiration and Motivation [3]

Inspiration and Motivation: Rationale or special purpose of a task or project that imparts meaning to the person working on it [3]

Intrinsic: by or in itself, rather than because of its associations or consequences; coming from within oneself [6]

Intrinsic reward: reward for performance or follow-through that comes from inside the person doing the task or by virtue of the nature of the task; rewards such as the good feeling when something is accomplished, sense of pride in work, knowledge that your work will benefit others, etc. [3]

Inverse leverage: the opposite of leverage; the loss of money, power, or ability to do some task well because some task or activity was not carried out properly. When inverse leverage occurs, the amount of loss is greater than anticipated due to synergistic effects. SEE LEVERAGE [3]

Investment: a contribution of something such as time, energy, or effort to an activity, project, or undertaking in the expectation of a benefit for oneself or others. [3]

Learning: acquisition of new facts or skills [6]

Leverage: the ability to increase ones ability to do work, make more money, or accomplish a task better by virtue of some supplementary activity, event, intervention, or factor. When leverage occurs, the amount of gain is greater than anticipated due to synergistic effects. When done correctly, delegation has a huge leverage factor. [2]

Open communication: free exchange of information and ideas. Open communication is important in organizational structures. [3]

Ownership: is a sense of purpose, responsibility, and authority a person delegated a task feels when they fully accept it as *their* task to accomplish [2]

Parameters: in the context of successful delegation, established and agreed upon boundaries or restrictions [3]

Peripheral people: people who are not directly charged with accomplishing a task whose services are necessary for its completion [4]

Process threats: threats to the delegation process that arise out of faults within the delegation process itself [8]

Psychological threats: threats to the delegation process that arise from within the delegater or the person being delegated to [8]

Purpose: the ultimate reason or rationale for doing a task. This goes beyond the rationale of it simply being assigned. If the purpose is strong [e.g. the school bus trapped behind a landslide], the impetus for doing the task, doing it well, and doing it on time increases. [3]

Reward: behaviorally speaking, any consequence of an action that increases that action; in the context of successful delegation, those extrinsic and intrinsic items or attitudes whose purpose is to thank the team member for her work and for successful follow-through of the task. [3]

Shared ownership: condition within an organization, group, or family where everybody takes responsibility for the successful operation of the system and everybody accepts responsibility for correcting errors that occur, the opposite of blame and seldom seen in most families. [3]

Transfer of knowledge: imparting of a core framework of understanding [6]

APPENDIX 1
MEET BILL AND JOANN TRUBY

BILL TRUBY

Bill Truby, M.A. MFCC, is a management consultant and educator   **121**
trained in psychology. Bill's focus is on improving the quality of
human fulfillment and performance in organizations. His clients
include architectural, engineering and design firms; manufacturing
companies, dental and medical offices, hospitals, wineries, insurance
companies, schools, health clubs, and various product, service and
sales organizations.

Bill's work includes consulting for goal setting, team building,
strategic planning, management transition; training in leadership,
communications, sales, delegation, motivation, and other organizational skills. His 5- Step Process For Organizational Success ensures
success in any organization.

Bill is a popular speaker and workshop leader for the American
Society of Landscape Architects, the Professional Services Manage-
ment Association, the American Society of Association Executives, the
Society of Architectural Administrators and the American Institute of
Architects.

He has worked extensively throughout the United States as well
as Australia, Singapore, Thailand and Hong Kong. Bill has a Master's
Degree in Psychology and has been teaching personal, interpersonal
and organizational success strategies for over 20 years.

JOANN TRUBY

Joann Truby is an experienced consultant, speaker, trainer, facilitator, and leadership coach. She has been a consultant to scores of businesses helping them become more successful. Her energetic speaking and training sessions not only provide attendees with meaningful, practical and usable information, she also motivates people to put into practice what she is teaching.

Joann has a broad-based perspective as a consultant, which qualifies her to help firms on many fronts. Her background and training enable her to coach success in everyday issues such as wellness, stress management, and time management. She also brings clients the ability to be successful in communication, leadership, conflict management and teamwork.

Joann aptly facilitates a variety of processes, from goal setting to having effective retreats. Her clients include architectural, engineering and related design profession firms; manufacturing companies, dental and medical offices, hospitals, wineries, insurance companies, schools, health clubs, and various product, service and sales organizations.

As a trainer, leader and educator, Joann's experiential and intuitive approach brings the clients of The Truby Achievement Center a powerful dimension of success. Those who experience her genuine, energetic spirit find motivation and a spirit of helpfulness that leads each individual to believe in the benefits of striving for personal success and balance in life—thus creating more personal fulfillment and corporate success.

One of Joann's unique and special talents is the ability to intuitively give input in training sessions. She knows exactly what to say and do to bring a group of people through a difficult spot or get through an impasse. She is a superior leadership coach. Many top leaders have found her training and coaching skills to be the life-changing ingredient that has enabled their growth and success. She has a rich and multi-faceted life experience where she has developed creative leadership skills and an intuitive ability to help individuals reach their fullest potential.

123

124

APPENDIX 2
WHAT THE TRUBY ACHIEVEMENT CENTER CAN DO FOR YOU

125

OUR STORY

The Truby Achievement Center is the place to find all the resources needed to help individuals and groups of people live life more abundantly and on purpose.

Through coaching, training, consulting, and facilitation, and by using a variety of books and training products, we help people achieve their goals. When a person or corporate group determines what goals they want to achieve, we either possess or create the tools and methodologies needed to reach that goal.

Our clients range from individuals seeking life-skills improvement to large corporations looking to grow. Our systematic approach focuses on simple, profound, manageable, core concepts and on systems that reap measurable results.

The Truby Achievement Center founders, managers and staff are caring people whose focus is to make a positive difference in other's lives. Integrity, inspiration, and "likeability" are the hallmark of their interactions with each other and their clients. The Truby Achievement Center environment is exhilarating with a constant sense of positive energy, power, growth, and success.

OUR MISSION:

To teach mental, physical, and spiritual success strategies that help you reach your fullest potential in your personal, interpersonal, and professional life!

OUR PROCESS:

We have systems, methodologies, and tools that enable any individual or group of individuals in any organization to achieve anything that does not violate a natural law. We do this by using principles of success that always create measurable difference!

Products & Services

Some of the proven, systemic processes that help organizations and individuals measurably increase their success are described below. We offer training, facilitation, and consulting in the following areas:

- Event Horizon (multi-day personal and professional development seminar)
- Communication training
- Personal Growth Intensive (PGI: three day intensive personal growth seminar)
- Coaching
- Executive coaching
- Conflict management training
- Corporate culture efficiency assessment
- Leadership and management assessment
- Leadership coaching
- Leadership and management training
- Process facilitation in any area including conflict, strategic planning, meetings and retreats
- Presentations training

- Stress management
- Soaring Eagles (personal growth for young adults)
- Team training (test your team at our website: www.teamworknow.com)
- The Truby Process (5-step business development)

Business and professional training and seminars are presented at your facility or a place of your choice. Personal growth seminars (Event Horizon and PGI) are usually held in Mount Shasta, California in a mountain setting near a view of one of nature's most wondrous and powerful places: Mount Shasta.

What we provide in all of our trainings, seminars, and services is *measurable difference.* If you don't get measurable difference from our work, then we haven't done our job!

Feel free to call and talk about these seminars and services or about any other "people and process" issues you may be facing. We stand ready to help!

CONTACT THE TRUBY ACHIEVEMENT CENTER:

Truby Achievement Center
P.O. Box 1440
Mt. Shasta, CA 96067
Phone: 1 (877) 377-3279 voice, fax, pager (*toll free*)
(530) 926-2328

Email us at: info@trubyachievementcenter.com

We trust that as a result of reading this book, you will be able to delegate successfully so that *you* can work more efficiently, more effectively and with less stress and strain on your relationships

128